Cambridge Elements

Elements in Early Christian Literature
edited by
Garrick V. Allen
University of Glasgow

THE AUTHOR IN EARLY CHRISTIAN LITERATURE

Chance E. Bonar
Tufts University

Shaftesbury Road, Cambridge CB2 8EA, United Kingdom

One Liberty Plaza, 20th Floor, New York, NY 10006, USA

477 Williamstown Road, Port Melbourne, VIC 3207, Australia

314–321, 3rd Floor, Plot 3, Splendor Forum, Jasola District Centre,
New Delhi – 110025, India

103 Penang Road, #05–06/07, Visioncrest Commercial, Singapore 238467

Cambridge University Press is part of Cambridge University Press & Assessment,
a department of the University of Cambridge.

We share the University's mission to contribute to society through the pursuit of
education, learning and research at the highest international levels of excellence.

www.cambridge.org
Information on this title: www.cambridge.org/9781009481380

DOI: 10.1017/9781009481397

When citing this work, please include a reference to the DOI 10.1017/9781009481397

First published 2025

A catalogue record for this publication is available from the British Library.

ISBN 978-1-009-48138-0 Hardback
ISBN 978-1-009-48140-3 Paperback
ISSN 2977-0327 (online)
ISSN 2977-0319 (print)

The Author in Early Christian Literature

Elements in Early Christian Literature

DOI: 10.1017/9781009481397
First published online: January 2025

Chance E. Bonar
Tufts University

Author for correspondence: Chance E. Bonar, chance.bonar@tufts.edu

Abstract: While scholars of ancient Mediterranean literature have focused their efforts heavily on explaining why authors would write pseudonymously or anonymously, less time has been spent exploring why an author would write orthonymously (that is, under their own name). This Element explores how early Christian writers began to care deeply about "correct" attribution of both Christian and non-Christian literature for their own apologetic purposes, as well as how scholars have overlooked the function that orthonymity plays in some early Christian texts. Orthonymity was not only a decision made by a writer regarding how to attribute one's own writings, but also how to classify other writers' texts based on proper or improper attribution. This Element urges us to examine forms of authorship that are often treated as an unexamined default, as well as to more robustly consider when, how, for whom, and for what purposes an instance of authorial attribution is deemed "correct."

Keywords: authorship, early Christianity, ancient Mediterranean literature, apologetics, book history

ISBNs: 9781009481380 (HB), 9781009481403 (PB), 9781009481397 (OC)
ISSNs: 2977-0327 (online), 2977-0319 (print)

Contents

Introduction

Interpretation of early Christian literature has often revolved around the figure of the author, with readers asking questions such as: who wrote this text? In what historical context(s) were they writing? What knowledge were they trying to transmit, and how should we interpret their words? The assignment of authors has at times functioned to solve the ambiguity of literary interpretation, allowing for statements like "this is what Paul says/thinks." Especially in the case of texts that have been labeled orthonymous (that is, correctly attributed to a named author), authorial attribution offers a sense of confidence that the author allows readers a window into a person's worldview or experiences.

In this Element, I argue in favor of contemplating the "window" of the author itself rather than rushing to look through it. We might see the author as a literary figure and a container for ideas, arguments, and relationships. The figure of the author is made useful for delineating the boundaries of acceptable knowledge, placing a text within a larger storyworld, or persuading an audience through demonstration of textual and authorial expertise. Authors can be added, omitted, overlooked, emphasized, and weaponized for different constructions of Christian history, polemic, and theology.

We tend to divide claims of authorship based on the presence of a name and the supposed historical accuracy of attaching the name to a specific text. Texts are labeled "orthonymous," "pseudonymous," or "anonymous" depending on whether the scholarly consensus holds that a particular historical figure did or did not write a given text. This tripartite division has cascading effects: for example, the proliferation of scholarship that explains why a writer would attribute their writing to someone else, or debates over authenticity (texts as "genuine" versus "forged"). The impulse to author-ize everything for the sake of modern classification leads to the attribution of tentative authors to anonymous texts; meanwhile, orthonymous texts and their authorial claims are often treated as an unexamined default.

My goal with this Element is to encourage further examination of authorship in the ancient Mediterranean world with an eye toward the obvious. The historical-critical and theological impulses to author-ize need not be the only approach to authors within early Christian studies. No less important, the reasons for *any* attribution of authorship deserves deeper scrutiny. I argue that orthonymity in particular needs to be explored in more depth to uncover who (whether in antiquity or modernity) chooses the "correct" author and what is at stake is that decision. While it is often taken for granted that it is "normal" to write in one's own name or attribute a text to the person who one believes to have written it, that normalcy is culturally determined and culturally contingent.

I do not aim to be comprehensive by any means in this Element, but rather to offer brief insights into a range of early Christian texts and into how orthonymity might affect the study of authorship and attribution in the ancient Mediterranean.

This Element has four sections. After a brief introduction to the study of authorship and orthonymity in the ancient Mediterranean, three case studies explore how debates over the "correct" author play out in antiquity and modernity through: (1) Paul's epistolary corpus; (2) Irenaeus and Tertullian's interaction with cento poetry; and (3) Eusebius's second-hand citations of Hellenistic Jewish authors via Alexander Polyhistor. These case studies highlight how the goals and assumptions of modern scholarship regarding authorship have often obscured the functions of orthonyms in early Christian literature.

Before going further, three caveats: The first is that my goal in this Element is by no means to historically verify the authenticity of any authorial claims, nor to claim that orthonymous attribution is the "best" or "right" way to organize and make sense of literature. I instead want to interrogate why orthonymity has often stood at the center (whether explicitly acknowledged or not) of modern scholarly interests, as well as complicate our treatment of such authorial figures. The second is that authorship – even "correct" authorship like (orth)onymity, defined in more depth in this Element – is not a monolithic phenomenon. Rather, we encounter a spectrum of possibilities and rationales for claiming that authorship has been rightly attributed. Sometimes an author writes something and attaches their own name to it; sometimes someone attaches the name of the person dictating a text; sometimes names or co-authors or collaborators are included or omitted; sometimes writers borrow or reuse textual material from other authorial figures; sometimes attribution of a text as orthonymous is done for apologetic, historical, or bibliographical purposes. The third point is related: what is deemed "correct" attribution of a text to an author is dependent upon the aims of those doing the work of attributing. As Jeremiah Coogan puts it in his analysis of early Christian conceptualizations of Gospel authorship: "authorial attributions are never independent, but are networked into broader imaginaries that develop in this transactional space."[1] As texts, readers, and their reading environments (and interpretative needs or hermeneutical frameworks) shift over time, attribution becomes "correct" or "incorrect" for different reasons. This Element is offered as an opportunity to consider how the relationship between orthonymous authorial attribution and correctness – whether historical or rhetorical – has been naturalized and might be disrupted by considering how all forms of attribution are a choice that someone makes.

---

[1] Coogan, "Imagining Gospel Authorship," 206.

1 Authorial Choices in the Ancient Mediterranean

Before exploring how authority plays out in early Christian literature, some historical and theoretical context is needed. What are the range of authorial possibilities in the ancient Mediterranean? What defines authorship, and how have various scholars theorized the role it plays in the production, interpretation, and circulation of texts? What, if anything, is so special about *orthonymity* – that is, the practice of attributing a text to the authorial figure deemed to have composed or dictated it? This first section lays the groundwork for understanding the variety of authorial attributions used by ancient writers, including a delineation of how the term and concept of "orthonymity" is used throughout this Element. The goal here is not to claim that each of these scholars offers the same understanding of authorship, but rather to demonstrate how the conversation has shifted within and beyond the field of early Christian studies as scholars critically analyze a range of authorial practices and norms.

Classical and early Christian studies have traditionally been invested in the determination of historically correct or incorrect attribution of authorship. Ostensibly, the goal was to prove that prominent figures of Mediterranean antiquity were involved in the literary production attributed to them – and, conversely, to prove if an individual had forged documents under a false name. As neatly stated by Eva Mroczek:

> We ask questions that reflect modern desires to establish authoritative texts, trace authorial attribution, and define relationships and hierarchies between texts. We want to fill in the blanks in our own knowledge of these texts, and complete our own fragmentary bibliographies; but we also project these interests onto ancient people themselves.[2]

While Mroczek is speaking here of modern scholarly concerns about the category of "scripture," her observation is relevant to how traditional historical-critical investigations are concerned with establishing "real" authors and valuing texts according to their assigned authorial status.

This historical argumentative framework can be found in biblical studies. For example, Bart Ehrman's *Forgery and Counterforgery* explored how early Christian writers produced texts under the names of prominent figures like Peter and Paul to justify their theological positions and gain an audience.[3] In response to scholars and the public who held that authorial claims of New Testament texts were historically accurate, Ehrman examined how and why early Christians resorted to "literary deceit" in their literary production – differentiated from what others have labeled as a "pious

---

[2] Mroczek, *The Literary Imagination*, 9–10.   [3] Ehrman, *Forgery.*

fraud."[4] Such scholarship in New Testament and early Christian studies often gravitates toward demonstration or rebuttal of particular historical claims: that Paul was or was not the author of Colossians, that Mark was or was not the author of the Gospel of Mark, that Peter was or was not the author of 1 Peter.

As David Brakke has rightly pointed out, scholarship that attempts to uncover the "historical author" is only one approach to authorship in antiquity, particularly if more recent discussions of the death and rebirth of the author are taken into consideration.[5] The French theoretical work of Roland Barthes, Michel Foucault, and Gérard Gennette have helped set the stage for new interventions in the study of ancient authorship and attribution and have allowed for questions beyond proving or disproving the accuracy of an authorial claim.

Roland Barthes's "The Death of the Author" combats the assumption in literary criticism that we can best understand any text through reconstructing the biography and original intentions of its author. This assumption proliferates in biblical studies, assuming that if we, for example, knew Luke's historical context and intentions in writing Luke–Acts, we would access to its most important interpretive layer. Against this assumption, Barthes suggests that the author is a fairly recent figure in the history of literature about which we are almost "tyrannically centered." He argues that this figure is unnecessary and nearly theological: the author is too often a god whose thoughts are taken as the final word.[6] Barthes's reader-response approach claims that it is the historical, biographical, and psychological context of the *reader*, not the *author*, where meaning is found. In other words, a text's unity is not "in its origin but in its destination" and an author can only ever return to a text they've written as a "guest."[7] Some argue that Barthes goes too far in rejecting the figure of the author without deeper analysis of the author's role in the production and interpretation of a text. Nonetheless, Barthes's attempt to "kill the author" highlights how texts can act and have meaning beyond the confines of their attributed authorial figures.

The death of the author is not without faults. Perhaps most notably, as Mark Jordan discusses in his work on Michel Foucault, the death of the author can dangerously mask the context in which the writer wrote.[8] To eradicate the author runs the risk of decontextualizing a text to such a degree that the author's

---

[4] See Speyer, *Die literarische Fälschung*, who proposed that an early Christian writer could genuinely believe they represent the thoughts of the figure whose name they wrote under.

[5] Brakke, "Early Christian Lies."

[6] Barthes, "Death of the Author," 277; Burke, *The Death and Return*, 22–25.

[7] Barthes, "Death of the Author," 280; Barthes, "From Work to Text," 239.

[8] Jordan, *Convulsing Bodies*, 6.

positionality is overlooked. Authors are also people; their embodiment and set of experiences impact what, how, and why they produce texts.[9]

Michel Foucault's 1969/1970 "What Is an Author?" is a counterbalance to Barthes's work, particularly through the coinage of the term *author function*. Foucault argued that an absolute death of the author would upend literary criticism, because even a core concept like a "work" could never be determined without the use of an author-figure or some other organizational feature to determine a text's boundaries and provide some meaningful context for encountering it.[10] Likewise, Foucault suggested that the concept of "writing" has subtly replaced the author without actually changing anything. In biblical studies and cognate disciplines, this approach is visible when the concept of authorial intent is quietly transferred to an anonymous "writer" or an idealized reader, to whom all interpretative authority is granted. For Foucault, the author often plays some role or function in how a text is interpreted, and urges readers to pay close attention to the particularities of an authorial figure.[11]

In short, Foucault argued that the attribution of a specific author both contextualizes texts and produces their boundaries. For example, attributing a text to Paul may activate author function to connect it to other "Pauline" texts, suggest that it falls under the epistolary genre, and place it within a mid-first-century Mediterranean itinerant preacher's storyworld. By "storyworld," I mean the narrative(s) that accumulate around particular individuals – especially through both textualized stories and attribution of texts to them – that shape how later generations of people perceive that individual.[12] Whether an *orthonym* or *pseudonym*, the authorial name of Paul is capable of linking one text to another and accumulating for the production of an authorial figure. The authorial "Paul" is never the same as the historical Paul or anyone else who writes in Paul's name: the figure of the author is born within and from the text itself.[13]

Foucault's analysis is unfortunately hindered since he thought that author function emerged only in the seventeenth and eighteenth centuries as a side-effect of the development of modern publication rights.[14] While such legal definitions of authorship and propriety differed in the ancient Mediterranean, concern over the authorship of a text and the implications was often evident. Galen's *On My Own Books*, for example, attest to such concerns. In this treatise, Galen takes aim at those who attribute books to him by attaching his name to

---

[9] Burke, "The Ethics of Signature," 237–244.   [10] Foucault, "What Is an Author?" 207.

[11] Foucault, "What Is an Author?" 211.

[12] See Lundhaug, "Pseudepigraphy," who deploys "biblical storyworld" for a similar purpose: To describe how Coptic pseudepigraphy functions to create and maintain particular narratives of individuals in the Bible for late ancient audiences.

[13] Birke, "Author, Authority, and 'Authorial Narration'."

[14] Foucault, "What Is an Author?" 212–213.

them, as well as those who received Galenic texts "without inscription" for friends or students who eventually pass his texts off as their own.[15] Galen's anxiety regarding the relationship between *text* and *authorial attribution* reveal the slipperiness of the publication process in the ancient Mediterranean: the possibility of multiple editions of texts circulating simultaneously, transferal of material deemed "wrong" via dictation or copying of manuscripts, or some texts (e.g., lecture notes) being treated as less ready for viewing or hearing by particular individuals than others.[16] Foucault's *author function* and Galen's concern over what he deems "improper" attribution of Galenic books both highlight two core questions for this Element: what work does a name do when attached to a text, and for whom do these attributions matter?

Literary theorist Gérard Genette's 1997 *Paratexts* further informs my approach to authorship, attribution, and orthonymity in early Christian litera- ture. Genette focuses on names, titles, and paratexts (i.e., material on the margins or apart from a text's main body). Like Foucault, Genette did not eradicate the figure of the author from the interpretative framework; rather, he asks that we consider the *function* of an author's name at the physical borders of a text.[17] Genette points to antiquity to demonstrate that there was often no location in which one could place an author's name besides the *incipit* of a text (e.g., "Herodotus" in *Histories* 1.1.pref). Eventually, writers begin to record their names elsewhere, often as part of distinct titles at the beginning or end of a text; for example, in the Hellenistic and Roman eras with the *sittybos* or *titulus* upon scrolls (a tag-like piece of papyrus attached to the scroll) that contained information about the text's title, number of books, and/or an authorial attribution.[18] Such tags – as paratextual information – contributed to the history of author function and organization of texts, allowing for easier arrangement of texts *by author* and requiring *some* authorial attribution in order to be "properly" stored. Genette also notes the importance of genre: some genres, like autobiography, require heavy-handed (orth)onymous authorial practices to be convincingly and meaningfully autobiographical; fiction, in contrast, does not require the same degree of onymity.[19] This approach is applicable also to biblical studies: the gospels are anonymous, epistles tend to have the names of sender(s) and recipient(s), apocalypses tend to be pseudepigraphic with some prominent exceptions (e.g., Revelation).[20]

While Genette focused primarily on the use of the author's name in modern books and did not take much interest in paratextual or authorial features in

---

[15] Galen, *Lib. prop.* K xix 9–10. Translation from Singer, *Selected Works*, 3.

[16] See Hanson, "Galen"; Singer, "New Light and Old Texts."   [17] Genette, *Paratexts*, 37.

[18] Bond, "It's on the Sillybos."   [19] Genette, *Paratexts*, 41.

[20] See Tóth, "Autorschaft und Autorisation," 11; Janßen, "Was ist ein Autor?" 98–100.

ancient or nonprint media, he offered a key term for my analysis of authorship: *onymity*. Genette splits this term into three concepts: a name that is not the author's own (*pseudonymity*), no name at all (*anonymity*), or their own name (*onymity*).[21] Genette pointed out that onymity is often overlooked because of how ordinary it is in Western literary culture, but that "to sign a work with one's real name is a choice like any other, and nothing authorizes us to regard this choice as insignificant."[22] We can apply this insight to ancient Mediterranean literature, since the decision to attach to a text one's own name or the purportedly "correct" name of another is a choice that impacts by whom and how the text is read, collected, preserved, and incorporated into storyworlds.

Scholarship of the last fifty years in early Christianity, early Judaism, and Classics have been influenced by French literary theory. Some recent works informs my approach to orthonymity across the range of authorial possibilities (i.e., pseudonymity, anonymity, onymity), and this scholarship has increasingly focused on why and how authorial attribution impacts the way that we read texts and organize literature.

Developments in technologies of attribution in the Hellenistic and Roman eras impacted how readers and libraries organized knowledge *by author*. Organization-by-author has been so normalized in our treatment of ancient literature that we often struggle to imagine other ways of classifying texts or knowledge. As noted by Ellen Muehlberger, classicists and religionists still "have an archive problem" because "the architecture of the knowledge we have inherited constrains what we think and write about."[23] She points in particular to the *Clavis Patrum Graecorum* system used by scholars to search for Greek Christian texts and its arrangement by author: in this framework, so-called pseudonymous texts enter an authorial limbo and can be overlooked. The commonality of our modern arrangement of early Christian literature by author is, in part, built upon a historical-critical desire to uncover and understand the "real" authors behind ancient texts. It highlights our normalization of orthonymity. The arrangement of encyclopedias, indices, and other search engines around orthonymous authorship both privileges scholarship on texts for whom we believe know the "real" author, and also presumes that early Christian writers ideally should have attached "real" names to texts.

This author-based classificatory scheme is attributed by Peter Martens to Jerome and his fourth-century *On Famous Men* (also entitled *On Ecclesiastical Writers* [*De scriptoribus ecclesiasticis*]). Jerome sets out to mimic non-Christian writers by providing a list and brief biography of "all those who have published

---

[21] Genette, *Paratexts*, 39–42 on onymity, 42–46 on anonymity, 46–54 on pseudonymity.
[22] Genette, *Paratexts,* 39. [23] Muehlberger, "On Authors, Fathers, and Holy Men."

any memorable writings on the holy scripture from the time of our Lord's passion until the 14th year of Emperor Theodosius (i.e., 393 CE)."[24] Jerome's biographical list spotlights those he deemed *authors* as prominent and memorable Christian writers, who need to have produced a text of some value beyond their initial audience or intent (by late fourth-century standards) as well as exist within a constructed "orthodox" ecclesiastical tradition. The centrality of (orth)onymity and authorial attribution as the conceptual scaffolding upon which Jerome categorized early Christian figures carried over to the modern era, where early Christian texts are still primarily classified based on authorial attribution, whether correct or incorrect (e.g., Pseudo-Ephrem, Pseudo-Chrysostom, Pseudo-Paul).

Building upon Muehlberger, Martens suggests that our current archive and its origins as a late ancient construction of an orthodox lineage of Christian authors simultaneously serves to help us "find what *special authors* wrote" and that "authorship also serves as a *hiding aid*" of texts and authors deemed heretical.[25] What Jerome and modern scholars who organized the *Clavis* have in common is a preference for "special authors" whose names are attached to texts that we believe were written by them. Authorship functions as a "hiding aid" not only in how it obscures other possible modes of classification (e.g., by genre), but even obscures how authorship generally and orthonymity in particular are treated as the classificatory norm. I want to extend Muehlberger and Martens's work on the normalization of authorship classification: it is particularly *orthonymity* that plays such a role, and so we must ask what would change if we place orthonymic practices and norms in the spotlight.

Before turning to orthonymity, it is worthwhile to note the important contributions regarding pseudonymity and anonymity that shape my understanding of authorship. The study of pseudonymity is something of a cottage industry.[26] Some scholarship on pseudepigraphy has sought to explain the rationale behind such authorial attribution. Rather than placing a value judgment upon a forged text,[27] some ask what function(s) the attached names serve in giving the text meaning or placing it within a particular tradition. Hindy Najman and Irene Peirano Garrison have suggested that we ought to disambiguate terms like "pseudepigraphy" from "forgery," given that the latter has a stronger negative connotation and involves an intent to deceive.[28] In its place, they suggest that pseudepigraphic literature might be better understood as "creative acts of

---

[24] Jerome, *On Famous Men*, pref. See Joost-Gaugier, "The Early Beginnings."

[25] Martens, "Classifying Early Christian Writings," 441, emphasis original. See also Breu, *Autorschaft in der Johannesoffenbarung*, esp. 152–241.

[26] For overviews, see Janßen, *Unter falschem Namen*; Waller, "The Erotics of Authenticity."

[27] Cueva and Martínez, ed., *Splendide Mendax*; Hopkins and McGill, ed., *Forgery beyond Deceit*.

[28] Najman and Peirano Garrison, "Pseudepigraphy," esp. 335n9, *contra* Ehrman, *Forgery*.

interpretation" developed in a literary culture invested in impersonation and continuity.[29] What makes pseudepigraphic texts interesting are not simply proving they are "wrongly" attributed, but exploring how ancient Mediterranean writers found value in connecting texts to authorial figures – narratives of law-giving sticking to Moses, revelation sticking to Ezra and Enoch, instruction and wisdom sticking to David and Solomon.[30] Such attribution is "correct" in a way that is unrecognizable within the limited bounds of historical criticism. Attribution was not solely used to arrange texts on a shelf, but to build bookish biographies of particular characters. While these examples are pseudepigraphic, the same can be said of orthonymous texts; they too work to create the *persona* of the author and their bookish biography.

Pseudonymity can also emerge within ancient pedagogical and exemplary models. As Kelsie Rodenbiker has argued, authorial figures like Peter became "reimagined for a Christian present and future," who represented ideal virtues or vices, and whose actions readers could emulate or avoid.[31] Likewise, educated Mediterranean writers learned how to mimic the literary styles of famous authors (e.g., Homer, Demosthenes), and such skills could be transferrable to produce authorial *personae* of well-known Christian figures.[32] We know that early Christians did this authorial role-playing through poems that respond to prompts like "what did Cain say when he killed Abel?" by offering an imagined oration from Cain.[33] As is exemplified by both the production of a "Peter"-author for 2 Peter and Christian poems exhibiting *ethopoeia* (the rhetorical impersonation of a character), early Christians participated in Greek and Roman pedagogical and rhetorical techniques in order to write in other voices and craft authorial *personae*.

Finally, Karen King's work on author function in Revelation and the *Secret Revelation of John* (*SRJ*) similarly interrogated how "the authority of Scripture is traditionally tied to authorship."[34] King suggested that we ought to pay attention to how attribution and author figures are deployed "to indicate the source of the work's contents, to guarantee stable transmission, and to situate the work within some broader context."[35] Such different types of deployment

---

[29] Najman and Peirano Garrison, "Pseudepigraphy," 343. See also Wyrick, *The Ascension of Authorship*, 83–104, who contrasts Greek valorization of individual authorial figures with ancient Jewish writers tending to de-emphasize individual composition and instead associating texts with prophets or prominent Israelite figures.

[30] See Najman, *Seconding Sinai*; Vayntrub, "Before Authorship"; Stuckenbruck, "The Epistle of Enoch."

[31] Rodenbiker, "The Second Peter."

[32] Cribiore, *Gymnastics of the Mind*, esp. 220–244; Bloomer, *The School of Rome*, esp. 170–191.

[33] Fournet, "Une éthopée de Caïn."   [34] King, "What Is an Author?" 15.

[35] King, "What Is an Author?" 18–19. Cf. Breu, *Autorschaft*, 159–179; Yoshiko Reed ("Pseudepigraphy, Authorship, and the Reception," 477) on how in Hellenistic Jewish compositions the "pseudonymous writer is not so much creator or author as tradent and guarantor."

need to be specified rather than covered under the umbrella term of "author" or "authorship": we have actions like recording, editing, composing, arranging, and more in which literary producers participate. While Revelation is often deemed orthonymous and *SRJ* pseudonymous, they use similar authorial strategies to claim that their texts originate from God, that they are trustworthy authorial intermediaries, and to place themselves within early Christian storyworlds.

Such scholarship on pseudepigraphy inspires this Element through its expansion of the functions of attribution and authorship, suggesting that modern philological and historical-critical interests in determining whether a text is genuine or forged may not always reflect the authorial concerns of ancient Mediterranean writers. Such work points to the importance of names and their power, and urges me to pay close attention to when names are evoked and what effects they might have.

Recent scholarship on anonymity, like pseudonymity, has furthered our understanding of ancient authorial practices in their historical context and in conversation with contemporary assumptions about author function. One of the most notable cases of anonymity are the four canonical gospels, attributed during the second century CE. Their anonymity is often treated as a troubling phenomenon by those who want author function to solidify a chain of transmission, a source of authority, and a proper place for them in the storyworld of early Christian figures. The gospel authors function as a lynchpin by which many modern (and late ancient) readers hope to securely identify the text's source and trust that it is meaningful for their lives as Christians, for their historical reconstruction of the early Jesus movement, or other purposes.[36] In response to the perceived oddity of anonymous gospel literature, some have offered rationales. For example, Armin Baum proposed that gospel literature built upon Near Eastern historical-literary practices, wherein writers attempted to remain "invisible behind the tradition he hands on, acting as its nameless mouthpiece."[37] By contrast, Robyn Faith Walsh has suggested that Mediterranean writers (especially of biography, paradoxography, and novels) used similar anonymizing practices at times that can explain gospel authorship. Walsh suggests that authorial anonymity and claiming divine knowledge are "strategies of authorization, not as evidence of oral tradition or communal speech [... and] are part of a larger trend toward 'anti-intellectualism' that becomes

---

[36] See Irenaeus's fourfold gospel defense (*Haer.* 3.11.8), Papias of Hierapolis on Mark and Matthew's composition of gospels, and Eusebius's explanation of gospel composition (*Hist. eccl.* 3.24).

[37] Baum, "The Anonymity," 137. Notably, John Chrysostom lamented the fact that we do not know the names of some authors in the Hebrew Bible (*Hom. in Rom.* 1.1; PG 60.395).

increasingly prevalent in the imperial period."[38] While not capable of proving that gospel texts represent communal histories or their later-named authors, anonymous author function can teach us about when authorial attribution was *not* deemed useful for their production or dissemination.

Tom Geue's *Author Unknown* also theorizes anonymous author(less) function, noting that because "Latin literature is littered with authors who want their names out there into infinity," we often struggle to make sense of those who consciously choose to be anonymous. Consequently, scholars have often assumed (just as some elite Romans did) that *orthonymity* is the norm and *anonymity* is a useless or accidental deviation.[39] An example from Lucian about a Knidian architect named Sostratos who hid his name on the Pharos tower (only to be revealed at a later point in time) encapsulates this assumption: Why write or produce anything if not for memorialization and prestige?[40] Kimberley Fowler has suggested that in some cases within early Christian literature, anonymity functions not simply to erase the author but "is an opportunity for the *reader* to put themselves in the same position as this unnamed disciple."[41] Anonymity may function to highlight the transmission of divine knowledge through a human vessel, protect authorial identities, or allow different actors to take center stage in a narrative. While my focus is on orthonymity, Walsh, Geue, and Fowler's scholarship urges me to pay attention to how both ancient and modern writers often treat anonymity as stripped-away-orthonymity. The presumption that texts only become anonymous by taking away an already-there name – originally included for what Cicero calls the universal "pursuit of fame" (*studio laudis*) – is one that can partially be undone by an examination of orthonymity on its own.[42]

Finally, we can turn to onymity and orthonymity. Kurt Aland first raised some of this Element's questions sixty years ago, when he lamented how scholarship failed to examine the difficulties that pseudonymity and anonymity caused for assigning early Christian literature to apostolic figures.[43] In response, he called on biblical scholars to more specifically note *when* and *under what circumstances* names of "real authors" were attached to texts by the mid-second century. Particularly in the case of early Christian apologists and heresiologists (e.g., Justin, Tertullian, Irenaeus, Hegesippus), he proposed a shift in the usefulness of orthonymity by the second century CE: some Christians wanted to be known and seen, and have their named attached to texts. Additionally,

---

[38] Walsh, *The Origins*, 137, also 155–169.   [39] Geue, *Author Unknown*, 7.

[40] Lucian, *Hist. Conscr.* 62; Geue, *Author Unknown,* 13–14.

[41] Fowler, "Divine Authorship," 460.   [42] Cicero, *Arch.* 26.

[43] Aland, "The Problem of Anonymity and Pseudonymity." Aland ties the growth of orthonymous Christian literature to the decline of prophesy and spirit possession in the second century (10–12).

Aland pointed to genre as a factor in authorial attribution, noting that "letters have to introduce their writers."[44] While Aland quickly conjured reasons why early Christian writers would want to remain unknown as authors – for example, to protect themselves from critique or to highlight the Holy Spirit's influence on their literary production – he pointed exactly to the concern of this Element:

> In my opinion we do not have to explain or to justify the phenomena of anonymity or pseudonymity in early Christian literature. It is the other way round: we need an explanation when the real author gives his name.[45]

I think Aland assumed too quickly that the rationales for pseudonymous and anonymous inscription have already been solved, but is correct that little justification has been offered for why some writers attribute a text with their own name. I add here that there is still a need to explain when and why early Christian writers started caring about the attribution of "correct" names to others' texts as part of their literary, historical, and apologetic projects.

Particularly in the Roman imperial era, classicists have begun to explore how writers use their own name in literary production. Karen Ní-Mheallaigh's work on Lucian, for example, demonstrated how Lucian plays with onymity as an almost-contractual obligation when writing orthonymously.[46] Lucian's author-ial *personae* are inversions of reflections of himself: Loukianos in the *True History* and *Peregrinus Proteus*, the Syrian in *The Dead Come to Life*, Lukinos in *Essays in Portraiture*.[47] Lucian's playful relationship between his orthon-ymous signature and his funhouse approach to truth-telling meddles with historical-critical approaches to authorship that equate orthonymity with the "real," historical individual behind the words on the page.[48] Even though such names are often considered to be "real" inasmuch as they refer to people in the world beyond the text and narration, Lucian's orthonyms work to expose the lack of clear relation between the authorial *persona* and the historical individual.

Similarly in her exploration of Roman poets, Irene Peirano Garrison built upon Genette's onymity to suggest that:

> the signature is perhaps the most visible and yet least examined mark of authorial presence. The deceptive simplicity and ordinariness of the author's referencing his own name [...] belies a complex and far from obvious nexus of functions associated with the author and revolving around issues of authentication, fiction, genre, and reception.[49]

---

[44] Aland, "The Problem of Anonymity and Pseudonymity," 3.
[45] Aland, "The Problem of Anonymity and Pseudonymity," 8.
[46] Ní-Mheallaigh, "The Game of the Name," 121.   [47] Whitmarsh, "An I for an I."
[48] Maciver, "Truth, Narration, and Interpretation."
[49] Peirano Garrison, "*Ille ego qui quondam*," 253.

Peirano Garrison suggested that attaching an orthonym to a text might work to make the narrative credible and to memorialize writers for future audiences.[50] Like Genette, she highlighted how orthonymity is treated as an unspoken, uncritiqued norm for how authors ought to identify themselves and their texts for many scholars of antiquity. Instead of treating (orth)onymity as the standard from which authors might deviate by erasing their name (anonymity) or replacing their name with another's (pseudonymity), attaching one's own name is a choice done for specific reasons. The signature is anything but a "straightforward conveyer of factual information," but is just as curated as any other form of authorial attribution.[51]

A helpful example regarding the development and theorization of a non-default orthonymity can be found in Benjamin Wright and Eva Mroczek's recent work on *Ben Sira* as pseudo-pseudepigraphy. Arguing against the consensus that *Ben Sira*, a second-century BCE Jewish instructional and moralizing text, was attributed to its actual writer because of Hellenic literary influence in the eastern Mediterranean, they propose that *Ben Sira*'s orthonymity emerged out of Jewish pseudonymous practices.[52] Along with suggesting that orthonymity needs just as much explanation as pseudonymity, they demonstrate that the writer of *Ben Sira* inserted their own name into a typically pseudonymous literary genre "that combines the idealization and memorialization of a figure over time and that figure's link to a developing textual tradition."[53] In other words, just as Ben Sira's grandson – who translated *Ben Sira* from Hebrew into Greek in the latter half of the second century BCE – placed his grandfather's book alongside "the law, the prophets, and other ancestral books, Ben Sira himself used orthonymity to craft his authorial *persona*. Using the norms of Jewish pseudepigraphic attribution, he positioned himself as one of the bookish Jewish ancestors, a "legendary exemplar and textual tradent."[54] Ben Sira's orthonymity is constructed out of the memorializing goals of Jewish pseudonymity, textual tradition, and memory-making.

Such scholarship encourages us to pay attention to what names are used and when, to ask what is gained by attaching one's own name to a text, to recognize that orthonymity is not necessarily (or even often) the norm in ancient Mediterranean literary production, and to more deeply interrogate our own assumptions about the relationship between an orthonym and the "real" person who wrote the text.

---

[50] Peirano Garrison, "*Ille ego qui quondam*," 255–256.

[51] Peirano Garrison, "*Ille ego qui quondam*," 253–254.

[52] Wright and Mroczek, "Ben Sira's Pseudo-Pseudepigraphy."

[53] Wright and Mroczek, "Ben Sira's Pseudo-Pseudepigraphy," 220.

[54] *Ben Sira* pref. 8–10 and Wright and Mroczek, "Ben Sira's Pseudo-Pseudepigraphy," 221, respectively.

Before moving on to my case studies, it is worth clarifying two distinct forms of orthonymity upon the spectrum of attributive practices. I'm calling these forms "intradiegetic orthonymity" and "extradiegetic orthonymity." Genette's narratological work proposed various levels of narrative (*diegesis* in Greek) at which narrators could function or be in relationship with the story that they told, ranging from homodiegetic, heterodiegetic, and autodiegetic to intradiegetic and extradiegetic.[55] The last two terms are most relevant to us here, and I'll explore each in turn.

"Intradiegetic orthonymity" borrows from narratological explorations of the *intradiegetic narrator*.[56] Intradiegetic narrators tell a story in which they play a role as a character, thereby functioning as both character and storyteller. Some ancient Mediterranean writers inserted themselves into the narrative (*diegesis*) as characters in the storyworld, thereby creating authorial *personae* who both narrate events and interact with other characters. We saw this earlier in the case of Lucian, who plays with the thin boundaries between narrator, character, author, and himself as a "real" person outside the text.

In early Christian literature, one of the clearest examples of intradiegetic orthonymity comes in the form of epistolary and dialogue literature. For example, Revelation opens with a third-person description of the text as "the revelation of Jesus Christ" (1:1) and then a first-person epistolary opening line from "I, John" (1:4). John of Patmos continues the narration after that point in the first person. In doing so, the writer of Revelation attributes the text to John of Patmos and positions John as author, narrator, and character in the visionary drama that God's angels reveal to him. Intradiegetic orthonymity functions also in the first- or second-century CE *Shepherd of Hermas*. Written from Hermas's first-person viewpoint, Hermas functions as the author who places his orthonymous *persona* into the text's storyworld through his conversations with divine figures like the Assembly and the angelic Shepherd. We will examine the complicated situation of the "Pauline epistles" in Section 2, but for now it suffices to say that Paul's authorial *persona* functions as an intradiegetic figure within that epistolary collection too.

Intradiegetic authorship allows us to distinguish between forms of attribution that happen *within the narrative itself* and *outside the narrative*. In the cases of Paul, John, and Hermas, each writer produced named authorial *personae* that scholars often associate with the "real," historical writers behind the text. One of the trickiest aspects of intradiegetic orthonymity in the ancient Mediterranean is that we are stuck either trusting that these writers put down their own name and/ or composed the words on the page. Cases have been made that "John of

---

[55] Genette, *Narrative Discourse*, 227–234.   [56] Nelles, *Frameworks*.

Patmos" and "Hermas" are pseudonyms, as well as that we cannot speak as securely about Paul being the (sole) authorial figure behind the words put down in his name.[57] We only ever encounter the literary output and *personae* such ancient authors created. Nonetheless, intradiegetic authorship helps us consider why some writers insert their own names and themselves as characters into texts they produce.

On the other end is what I am calling "extradiegetic orthonymity." Attribution of "correct" authorship often occurs through a paratext or *extradiegetic* figure who narrates and/or assigns authorship from outside of the storyworld. Genette defined a *paratext* as the pieces of writing that orbit the main text (e.g., titles, marginal notes, prefaces).[58] Paratextual material shapes, contains, and contextualizes the material held within, and have increasingly become a focus of early Christian scholars as we explore the margins and physicality of manuscripts.[59] Foucault's concept of author function focuses especially on paratextual forms of authorship: attaching one's name to a book manuscript or to a title page without incorporating the authorial *persona* into the narrative itself. Importantly, paratextual material impacts how one encounters the main text. As Florian Sedlmeier has argued, "the paratext is not just a supplement to the text, or a strategy to secure its publication in the format of a book, but also part of the practices of narrating, even a narrative element in its own right."[60] We see this in how titles attached at the beginning or end of pages on some extant early Christian papyri. Even subtle differences, like the titles of texts like the *Gospel of Judas* (ⲡⲉⲩⲁⲅⲅⲉⲗⲓⲟⲛ ⲛ̄ⲓⲟⲩⲇⲁⲥ) versus the *Gospel according to Mary* (ⲡⲉⲩⲁⲅⲅⲉⲗⲓⲟⲛ ⲕⲁⲧⲁ ⲙⲁⲣⲓϩⲁⲙⲙ), alter how one encounters the text contained within as being *about* a particular figure or being written *by* a particular author.[61] The same might be said of the *syttiboi* discussed earlier, as booktags that can mark authorial attribution for a bookroll and provide information for someone searching for a particular bookroll on a shelf. Having a name like "Homer" or "Vergil" attached to a *syttibos* frames how someone will read the text contained within as Homeric or Vergilian – which we will explore more in Section 4.

Extradiegetic orthonymity is often signaled allographically (i.e., by someone other than the author), most commonly in early Christian literature through the later attribution of authorship to an anonymous text. For example, *1 Clement*, an anonymous first-/second-century CE letter from the Roman Christian assembly to the Corinthians, became paratextually attributed to Clement in manuscripts

---

[57] Frey, "Das Corpus Johanneum"; Joly, *Le Pasteur*, 17–21; Moss, "What Large Letters."

[58] Genette, *Palimpsests*, 3.   [59] Allen and Royle, "Paratexts Seeking Understanding."

[60] Sedlmeier, "The Paratext and Literary Narration," 69.

[61] See Larsen, "Correcting the Gospel" on the tradition of κατά + person or κατά + city authorial ascriptions.

and extradiegetically attributed to Clement by later writers like Dionysius of Corinth and Eusebius, who referred to it as an "epistle, which was written to us through Clement" or "Clement's epistle to the Corinthians."[62] This type of attribution of a "correct" author is most relevant for Section 4, in which I explore Eusebius (via Alexander Polyhistor) transmits Hellenistic Jewish figures who are often deemed orthonymous authors. Inasmuch as we have access to their writings through other writers, such attribution of orthonymity occurs outside of the bounds of their own texts.

Both methods of orthonymity draw our attention to the specifics of how and where authorial attribution occurs – how authors wrote a *persona* of themselves into narratives, how scribes and editors mark off texts in the blank space of a papyrus with authorial claims, how later writers construct literary biographies around texts in order to link them to certain authorial figures. (Orth)onymity is a phenomenon that can be activated or claimed both internally and externally, but in every case involves a series of decisions regarding how to connect a text to a name.

The goal in this section has been to lay out some of the basics of orthonymity within the broader context of authorship and attribution in the ancient Mediterranean. Ancient orthonymity is notably underexplored in relation to pseudonymity and anonymity, in large part because it is the invisible center of modern Western literary practices. Nevertheless, orthonymity is a choice rather than a default, whether applied to a text by the writer itself or by someone else. As we will see in this Element, orthonymous attribution is sometimes disguised, sometimes misleading, sometimes polemical, and sometimes incidental. Nonetheless, each attribution of a text to the name of the writer who purportedly produced it does specific types of work: it can place a text within a particular storyworld, can connect various texts that have the same authorial name, or function to bolster the credibility of claims contained within.

2 Coauthorship and Literate Labor in the Pauline+ Epistles

The multiple letters attributed to Paul compiled in the New Testament are typically classified as a (somewhat) coherent group of literature: the "Pauline epistles." Scholars often speak of them as representing Paul's voice and/or Pauline thought, and examine these letters to better understand how Paul developed as an itinerant preacher and teacher in the mid-first century CE.[63] Given the divergence in thought and practice that the epistolary Paul advocates

---

[62] Eusebius, *Hist. eccl.* 4.23.11; 3.16.

[63] Schreiner, *Interpreting the Pauline Epistles*. For a challenge to Paul's centrality, see Marchal, *Bodies on the Verge*.

for between letters like 1 Thessalonians and 1 Timothy, scholars have divided up the thirteen letters attributed to Paul into two camps: genuine Pauline epistles and pseudo- or deutero-Pauline epistles. Such scholarship suggests that narrowing the range of texts attributed to an "historical Paul" brings us one step closer to understanding Paul's conception of communal practices, crisis management techniques, Jewish scriptural interpretation, and more. In this section, I want to add a layer of complexity to the discussion of the authorship and role of slavery in the Pauline+[64] epistles by asking about an often-overlooked feature of many letters attributed to Paul: named coauthorship.

Most of the letters that scholars deem genuinely Pauline are coauthored, and yet the author function of Paul's coauthors is underexplored. What does it mean for Paul to write letters with other people? How is coauthorship rhetorically displayed (or not) in texts that we have traditionally called "Pauline"? What if Paul is not the "Great Man" and sole author(ity) behind epistles that bear his name?[65] Orthonymity and coauthorial attribution is purposefully done, such that *orthonym function* and *coauthor function* require explanation. My goal here is to explore the function of Pauline coauthors in the letters in which they purportedly play some role. Scholarship building upon Antoinette Clark Wire's examination of the Corinthian women prophets – to whom Paul responds in 1 Corinthians – has demonstrated that it is, in fact, possible to decenter and displace Paul within the collection of letters traditionally attributed to him.[66] Decentering Paul may also involve recognizing the literary and authorial labor of others involved in his epistolary output.

To begin, I will discuss Paul's named coauthors and the history of scholarship around them. Scholars tend to treat Paul's coauthors on a spectrum of literary influence, between having no tangible impact on coauthored epistles and having a notable influence on some aspects. Then, I will contextualize Pauline+ coauthorship in contemporaneous Mediterranean practices of coauthored writing. Finally, I will turn more fully to the issue of orthonymity and Pauline+ coauthorship to ask what might change in our reading of 1 Corinthians. My hope is that such a discussion will challenge readers to reconsider how Pauline+ epistles present literary and epistolary collaboration, as well as what historical, literary, and theological assumptions we bring with us when encountering Pauline+ texts. There are more writers and thinkers in the "Pauline epistles" than we thought; their author function does something *to* the letters and *for* the letters that goes beyond Paul alone.

---

[64] I add the + to disrupt the way that this is often deemed a monoauthored and univocal "Pauline" collection, even among the seven "genuine" epistles.

[65] Stillinger, *Multiple Authorship*; Concannon, *Profaning Paul*.

[66] Wire, *The Corinthian Women Prophets*; Marchal, *After the Corinthian Women Prophets*.

Let us begin with an introduction to the three main named figures that constitute Paul's epistolary coauthors: Sosthenes, Silvanus, and Timothy. Scholars have traditionally conceived of them as participating (or not) to various degrees in Paul's literary repertoire. In his account of Paul's use of secretaries, E. Randolph Richards concludes by noting that "it is not acceptable to sideline the issue [of Paul's secretarial use] and proceed as if the letters were solely the words and thoughts of Paul."[67] Here, I suggest we share the same concern for Paul's coauthors, whose role in the production of Pauline+ correspondence – as well as how *coauthor function* is activated – is often downplayed or ignored.

To examine coauthors involves considering the legal and social status of these figures. Recent scholarship by Candida Moss has highlighted how enslaved and formerly enslaved literate labor was central to the composition, editing, copying, and distribution of New Testament literature.[68] I agree wholeheartedly that enslaved and formerly enslaved literary workers constituted much of Paul's epistolary workforce and ought to be recognized as omitted authorial figures. In this section, I focus my attention not on the enslaved literary workers whose presence and contributions have been made invisible, however, but on the visible-and-still-overlooked presence of *named* coauthorial figures. Even as the presence of named coauthors works to disguise the labor of other enslaved literate workers involved in the production of these epistles, they offer one angle by which disrupt the narrative of Paul's singular voice.

Sosthenes is described, either by Paul or by himself, as "the brother" in 1 Corinthians 1:1 and is Paul's only coauthor for this letter. Some suggest that the Sosthenes of 1 Corinthians is the same person as the head of the synagogue named Sosthenes in Acts 18:17, while others see him as a previously unknown travel companion.[69] As Jerome Murphy-O'Connor has summarized, many scholars argue that Sosthenes is not truly a coauthor, offered little substance to the letter, functioned as a memory aid, or merely is named to demonstrate that he is in agreement with Paul's line(s) of argumentation.[70] Sosthenes is often characterized as a subordinate coworker, whose role in the text of 1 Corinthians and Paul's ministry more broadly is almost secretarial or superficial.

Such arguments fit with an even broader consensus that holds Paul's authorial genius on a pedestal and treats it as virtually untouchable. Sosthenes cannot be imagined as a contributor to 1 Corinthians in part because this would cause

---

[67] Richards, *The Secretary*, 201.   [68] Moss, *God's Ghostwriters*, 50–87, esp. 69–79.

[69] Hubbard, "Urban Uprising in the Roman World"; Fee, *The First Epistle*, 31. Likewise, some late ancient Christians presumed that this was the same Sosthenes, such as John Chrysostom (PG 60.278), Theodoret of Cyrus (PG 82.229) and Oecumenicus (PG 118.244–640).

[70] Murphy-O'Connor, "Co-authorship," 566–567, pointing to Fee, *The First Epistle*, 30–33; Klauck, *1. Korintherbrief*, 17.

hermeneutical complications for modern readers (e.g., "was it *Paul* or *Sosthenes* who wrote this verse?") and because it disrupts the tidy classificatory boxes used for "genuine" and "forged" Pauline letters. Additionally, it is likely that Sosthenes was an enslaved or formerly enslaved literate worker whom Paul makes use of for this letter, involved in the editing, composition, and/or receiving of dictation from Paul.[71] The possibility of coauthors complicates claims of a coherent Pauline thought that can be uncovered through stylistic or textual analysis, since what we might find instead is a set of different rhetorical strategies between coauthors as they bounce back and forth between each other, or between singular and plural epistolary speakers. Murphy-O'Connor has begun such work by arguing that Sosthenes's authorial presence is most explicit in 1 Cor 1:18–31 and 2:6–16.[72] In opposition to claims that the "we" of 1 Corinthians 1–2 is a "common editorial we" or an earlier source used by Paul and Sosthenes, Murphy-O'Connor suggested that 1:18–31 and 2:6–16 are "theoretical arguments on the level of principle" offered by Sosthenes, and that Paul interjects with his own first-person voice twice (2:1–5 and 3:1–4) out of impatience with "the somewhat diffuse sophistication" of Sosthenes's thoughts.[73] We may, in fact, have free and (formerly) enslaved voices seeping through what is presumed to be a univocal text.

We also encounter another coauthor alongside Paul and Timothy in 1–2 Thessalonians who may have been an enslaved or formerly enslaved literate worker: Silvanus.[74] Silvanus appears in 1 Thess 1:1 and 2 Thess 1:1 alongside Paul and Timothy as a writer, but also among the same two figures as a preacher in 2 Corinthians 1:19. The writer of 1 Peter also claims to have written to the diasporic communities in Asia Minor "through Silvanus, a loyal brother to you as I consider him" (5:12).[75] While it is not immediately obvious that 1 Peter's Silvanus is the same as that of 1–2 Thessalonians, some have noted shared terminology between the letters that might link them to a shared Silvanean character.[76] Silvanus is occasionally also identified with Silas, who appears at the Jerusalem council in Acts 15 as a prophet and coauthor of the letter to eastern Mediterranean gentiles.[77]

---

[71] See *CIL* VI 29681 for an example of Sosthenes as a freedperson's name. For these various literary roles, see Moss, *God's Ghostwriters*, 36–44 and 72–75.

[72] Murphy-O'Connor, "Co-authorship," 567–570.

[73] Murphy-O'Connor, "Co-authorship," 569–570. Opposing claims can be found in Ellis, *Prophecy and Hermeneutic*, 26.

[74] For examples of Silvanus as a name for enslaved and formerly enslaved persons, see *CIL* II 3336; *CIL* VIII 12607; *CIL* IX 219.

[75] Richards, "Silvanus Was Not Peter's Secretary" argues that Silvanus must have been a letter-carrier. For Silvanus as a scribe, see Vaught and Lea, *1, 2 Peter, Jude*, 132.

[76] Sargent, "Chosen through Sanctification."   [77] Achtemeier, *1 Peter*, 349–352.

Compared to Sosthenes, Silvanus is given a bit more credit by scholars as a coauthor whose voice is meaningful for 1–2 Thessalonians, because both letters predominantly use first-person plural language throughout, with only rare first-person singular interjections by Paul and/or others. Silvanus is not named again in 1 Thessalonians, but only appears in the use of "we" throughout. By contrast, Paul makes a few individual appearances in the letter, particularly in 2:18 when he interjects and notes his intense desire to visit the Thessalonians: "Therefore we wanted to come to you – certainly I, Paul, [did] over and over." Here we find Paul not only interrupting his coauthors, but adding his own name to clarify who the "I" is that so strongly wants to be in Thessalonica. This point will become important later in this section: the orthonymic use of "I, Paul" suggests that Paul occasionally clarifies that *he* is the "I" who is speaking. Doing so suggests that readers of Paul's letters may not have always assumed that *Paul* is the "I" who interjects.[78] The other two interjections that break the plural norm of 1 Thessalonians appear in 3:5 and 5:27. The former is an "I" – either Paul or Silvanus – who claims to have sent Timothy to learn about the Thessalonians' loyalty, taking full credit for the "we" who sent Timothy to them in 3:2. The latter instance also contains an ambiguous "I" who commands that 1 Thessalonians be read to the siblings present among the recipients.

The case of 2 Thessalonians is slightly trickier, given that scholarly consensus tends to view it as a pseudepigraphic letter. The letter claims the same three coauthors as 1 Thessalonians (i.e., Paul, Timothy, Silvanus) and mimics its plural writing style, only interjecting with a singular authorial figure twice: an "I" who claims to have previously taught the Thessalonians about the coming man of lawlessness (2:5) and an "I" who claims to be Paul that nearly exaggerates their authorial presence: "The greeting with my own hand – Paul, which is my sign in every letter. I write this way" (3:17). The Paul of 2 Thessalonians leans heavily into the claim that the written presence of the name Παῦλος certifies this and other letters as being written by Paul.[79] That is, the writer presumed that the orthonym functions to secure 2 Thessalonians's transmission as a Pauline epistle and place it within his repertoire.

The coauthorship of 1–2 Thessalonians is not always seen as obvious. Adolf Harnack, for example, found it preposterous that Timothy could speak in the plural first-person about "we" sending himself to Thessalonica (1 Thess 3:2).[80] Likewise, C. E. B. Cranfield argued that the "we" of 1–2 Thessalonians was comparable to a "royal we" or a first-person singular disguised as a plural – despite how a previous generation of scholars had convincingly demonstrated

---

[78] Cf. Prior, *Paul the Letter-Writer*, 39–40.   [79] Ehrman, *Forgery*, 170–171.
[80] Harnack, *Die Briefsammlung*, 12.

that Paul was comfortable jointly authoring his earlier letters.[81] Others like Leon Morris claimed that 1–2 Thessalonians cannot be truly coauthored because they are too stylistically similar to other (mostly coauthored) Pauline epistles, such that coauthorship with Paul must have been "largely a matter of courtesy."[82] Argument from courtesy, however, does not hold up well since it fails to explain why Paul would include some people as named coauthors, but not other figures who are explicitly noted to be present with him at the time of composition.[83] Additionally, erasure of enslaved or formerly enslaved literate workers perpetuates misunderstandings about the role of enslaved labor in the production of New Testament literature.

Timothy is the most involved of Paul's coauthors.[84] He appears alongside Paul and Silvanus as author of 1–2 Thessalonians, as well as alongside Paul in 2 Corinthians, Philippians, Philemon, and Colossians. Murphy-O'Connor has explored Timothy's role as coauthor in 2 Corinthians, arguing against assertions that Timothy's authorial presence is merely a façade meant to approve of Paul's message or rehabilitate Paul for a Corinthian audience.[85] We also see implicit demotions of Timothy's influence in many academic treatments of 1 Thessalonians through claims that his coauthorial status refers merely to his role as a letter-carrier, since Timothy is often the figure sent by Paul to handle communities in his stead.[86] Such a characterization ignores how literate labor often depended on enslaved and formerly enslaved persons functioning in multiple areas of literary competency: composition, editing, reading, receiving dictation, and physically carrying messages. Even those who imagine Timothy as coauthor often do not sustain a coauthorial Timothy through their entire examination of the letter, but treat coauthorship as a formality that can be dismissed while excavating Pauline theology and first-century Christian history.[87]

Finding a context for named coauthorship in the ancient Mediterranean is a difficult task. E. Randolph Richards, for example, argued that there were two broad categories of coauthored letters in antiquity: (1) those written in a group's

---

[81] Cranfield, "Changes of Person and Number." *Contra* arguments for coauthorship by Askwith, "'I' and 'We'"; Lofthouse, "Singular and Plural"; Lofthouse, "'I' and 'We'."

[82] Morris, *The First and Second Epistles*, 46–47.

[83] Richards, *Paul and First-Century Letter Writing*, 34.

[84] For examples of Timothy as a (formerly) enslaved person's name, see *CIL* X 6514; *CIL* VI 7009; *CIL* VI 8917.

[85] Murphy-O'Connor, "Co-authorship," against Furnish, *II Corinthians*, 104. Malina (*Timothy*, 79–94) briefly examines Timothy as cowriter, but mines the letters for sociohistorical data points about Timothy rather than examining his role in the production of the epistles.

[86] Wannamaker, *The Epistles to the Thessalonians*, 68.

[87] As noted in Richards, *Paul and First-Century Letter Writing*, 35. For example, Bruce, *1 & 2 Thessalonians*, xi; Fee, *The First and Second Letters*, 30.

name to a governmental figure to solve a problem, or; (2) a situational letter to a spouse.[88] He pointed to six examples from Oxyrhynchus, Tebtunis, and the Zenon archive as evidence of coauthorship's rarity. Additionally, he argued that coauthorship was functionally a "Christian phenomenon," since according to him elite Roman authors like Pliny, Cicero, and Seneca did not coauthor texts.[89] Such a line of argumentation gives the impression that Paul innovated by including coauthors.

By contrast, Murphy-O'Connor has suggested that we cannot dismiss coauthorship as if it were a virtually unknown aspect of ancient Mediterranean epistolary habits. As he points out, Cicero both knew of and participated in coauthored letter-writing. For example, when writing to Atticus, Cicero notes that he gathered two types of Atticus's letters: "both those that you wrote in conjunction with others (*quas communiter cum aliis*) and those you wrote in your own name (*quas tuo nomine*)."[90] This example not only demonstrates Cicero's knowledge of cowritten letters, but that *cowriting* was deemed distinct from writing *in one's own name*; it is part of an expansive conceptualization of "correct" authorial attribution. It is unclear if Cicero's collection of Atticus's coauthored letters were anonymous collective documents or had specific coauthorial orthonyms attached.[91] In either case, however, Cicero deems Atticus's coauthored letters *not* to be in his own name, which might raise questions about whether we might reconceptualize Paul's coauthored letters as *not (exclusively) in Paul's name*. Such attribution may be "correct" without being orthonymous.

Beyond this example, Murphy-O'Connor points to a set of coauthored letters within Cicero's *familia*.[92] In a few of these cases, Cicero and his son Marcus coauthor letters to Cicero's wife Terentia and daughter Tullia. Like some of Paul's letters, Cicero and Marcus open with first-person plural language ("If you are well, we are well" [*si vos valetis, nos valemus*]), but quickly switch to a first-person singular "I" who does most of the talking.[93] The same thing occurs in a letter sent a day earlier, where Cicero's authorial "I" dominates the correspondence until a final "us" (*vos*) representing he and Marcus is evoked to remind Terentia and Tullia to stay healthy.[94] The rest of Cicero's coauthored letters are addressed to his (formerly) enslaved literate worker, Tiro. Of these, most are coauthored by Cicero, Marcus, and the two Quinti (Cicero's brother and nephew), and they share similar features with Cicero's letters to Terentia

---

[88] Richards, *Paul and First-Century Letter Writing*, 33.

[89] Richards, *Paul and First-Century Letter Writing*, 33–36, 47n138.   [90] Cicero, *Att.* 11.5.1.

[91] Richards (*Paul and First-Century Letter Writing*, 34n9), for example, asks whether Atticus's coauthorial practice falls into his category of corporate entities cowriting to a governmental entity for a solution or support.

[92] Murphy-O'Connor, "Co-authorship," 563.   [93] Cicero, *Fam.* 14.14.1 (145.1).

[94] Cicero, *Fam.* 14.18.2 (144.2).

and Tullia.[95] Despite their coauthorship, these letters tend toward a Ciceronian "I" who is constantly worried about Tiro's health and his ability to recover and leave Patrae. Even in Cicero's most robustly coauthored letter – himself, Marcus, Terentia, Tullia, and the two Quinti to Tiro – their writing is replete with Cicero's "I," his itinerary, and his concern for Tiro.[96]

Cicero's ego does not mean, however, that he never recognizes that his coauthors exist. When informing Tiro about his location alongside Marcus and the Quinti, they let slip a few cases of "we" and "us" (*nos*) to describe their stay in Alyzia. However, Cicero interjects multiple times to inform Tiro of when he sent letters the day before, when he will send letters tomorrow, and to beg Tiro (twice!) to "love us all but especially me, your master" (*nos omnis amas et praecipue me, magistrum tuum*).[97] Cicero also distinguishes between singular and plural when writing alone to Tiro, noting that "we" (i.e., Cicero and Marcus) stayed as Alyzia until Quintus arrived the next day, and that the same "we" were stuck in Corcyra while the Quinti were in Buthrotum.[98] Cicero occasionally allows his coauthors' presence to be known, but in a much rarer and more selective way than how Paul's coauthors (dis)appear. Cicero's curated epistolary collection is not the perfect comparand for Paul's coauthorial proclivities, but can function as a helpful foil – as an *ego* who lets his ego get in the way of other authorial figures, as a writer who demonstrates that he knows the meaning of *nos* but mitigates its presence in coauthored letters.

As noted earlier, Richards examined 645 papyrus letters and found only six that were explicitly coauthored,[99] which led to his argument that: (1) coauthored epistles are primarily a Christian innovation, and (2) little comparative work can be done between "pagan" and Pauline coauthored correspondence. However, this rarity of coauthored correspondence is partially manufactured because Richard sought out instances of coauthorship in elite correspondence. Perhaps the largest base of overlooked coauthored letters are the various ostraca and papyri relating to payment of taxes of debts. Although I do not provide a comprehensive list here, I hope that this demonstrates that there are other types of Greek correspondence that can be comparatively examined.

A substantial amount of coauthored correspondence is sent by or to tax collectors, sometimes with only one of their names listed (which partially explains why they have been overlooked) and occasionally with two or more names. For example, BGU 6.1453, an early Ptolemaic letter from 325 BCE

---

95 Cicero, *Fam.* 16.1 (120); 16.3 (122); 16.4 (123); 16.5 (124); 16.6 (125).
96 Cicero, *Fam.* 16.11 (143).   97 Cicero, *Fam.* 16.3.1–2 (122.1–2).
98 Cicero, *Fam.* 16.2 (121); 16.7 (126); 16.9 (127).
99 Richards, *Paul and First-Century Letter Writing*, 33–36, listing primarily second- and third-century letters: P.Oxy. 2.118, 8.1158, 9.1167, 42.3064, 43.3094, 46.3313, and maybe P.Zen. 35.

written on an ostracon, contains correspondence from Tauron, Psenchonsis, and "their partners" (οἱ μέτοχοι) to someone whose name is partially lost (Petousiris Arka[…]s) with instructions to deliver two loads of chaff as a tax payment. Another ostracon from second-century CE Thebes records "Petechespouchrates and his tax-collector partners of the treasury of holy ones" writing a receipt for a bath-tax to Psenamounis.[100] Such letters were plentiful in Ptolemaic and Roman Egypt, with tax-collectors and other μέτοχοι of the local *agoranomos* meticulously documenting, requesting, and providing receipts for a range of transactions: sales-tax payments on enslaved people, weaver's taxes, taxes on camp marketplaces, poll taxes, court fees, harbor taxes, and payment to public bankers.[101] Many similar letters request that the recipient pay a certain amount to their partner upon arrival.[102] Still others are registers of sale for a house or land, or record a transaction between two parties within which two or more people are present in one party.[103] There are also a few examples of coauthored correspondence in military contexts, such as the letter from Niger and Brocchus to Flavius Cerialis, prefect of the ninth cohort of Batavians at the Roman British military fortress of Vindolanda.[104] The predominant form of coauthored correspondence in the Hellenistic and Roman periods appears to be neither Richards's collective letter to a governmental official nor letters to family, but correspondence regarding taxes, payments, and economic exchange. Coauthored letters may not be as rare as previously thought, but rather scholars were looking for them in the wrong places.

Early Christian letters like Polycarp of Smyrna's letter to the Philippians are written from multiple authors as well, sent from "Polycarp and the elders with him" to the Philippian *ekklēsia*.[105] Most of the letter, like those cowritten with Cicero, are filled with first-person singular statements and exhortations, even claiming that "I am writing […] not on my own initiative but because you invited me to do so" and that Polycarp's letters are but a pale imitation of Paul's.[106] Polycarp's *Philippians* is, in fact, a good imitation of Paul's letter to

---

[100] O.Amst. 46. See also *2 Macc* 11:34 and Josephus, *Ant.* 12.5.5, 13.3.1–2 for examples of coauthored letters by the Judaeans, Samaritans, and Ptolemy VI with Cleopatra II.

[101] P.Oxy. 1.185; P.Tebt. 1.37; O.Ashm. 43–44; O.Ash.Shelf 17; O.Berenike 2.140; O.Berl. 27, 47; O.Bodl. 2.569; O.Wilcken 2.801; SB 1.4333, 5.7570, 16.13003, 18.32279, 18.14031, 22.15387; UPZ 2.172; ZPE 209.217.

[102] O.Bodl. 1.251 (Asklepiades and Gorgias to Paloutis regarding payment to their partner Ptolemaios); PSI 15.15153 (Tryphon to Aryotes regarding owing Patunis and his partners nine arouras).

[103] O.Cair. 89 (Kalasiris of Horus and his partners regarding payment for a funeral-related object); P.Oxy. 78.5176 (Heraclides and Ammonius to an *agoranomos* regarding a register of sale for a house and courtyard, undersigned by Polemon and his μέτοχοι); SB 12.11145 (sent to Dionysius and his fellow keepers of the grain).

[104] Tab.Vindol. I 21 (no. 248).   [105] Pol. *Phil.* 1.1.   [106] Pol. *Phil.* 3.1–2.

Philippians in the sense that he gives little space for his coauthors to have a voice around the immensity of the Polycarpian ego. Polycarp also exemplifies the early process by which writers crafted a monoauthorial Pauline corpus, since claims that Paul was both present with the Philippians and that "he wrote letters" (ἔγραψεν ἐπιστολάς). Such an assertion works to erase Timothy's coauthorship in the process – although Paul himself had already started this process.[107] The uses of "we" that Polycarp deploys (especially from 5.1–8.2) refer not solely or explicitly to the "we" of coauthorial presbyters, but rather address the readership of Polycarp's letter within a more encompassing "we-circle."[108] Only once do the presbyters make an appearance near the end of the epistle, when "we are sending to you the letters of Ignatius that were sent to us by him, and any others we have with us."[109] For this brief moment, other authors peek through as providers of textual information and embodied bridges between the teachings of Ignatius and the Philippian community. Like with Pauline+ epistles, Polycarp's letter to the Philippians has traditionally been analyzed as a monoauthored text and has not examined in depth why and under what conditions other authors are evoked.[110]

This short run-through of coauthored correspondence in the Hellenistic and Roman periods is by no means comprehensive, but is meant to demonstrate that coauthored texts are not as uncommon as has often been presumed. We see here a range of coauthorial strategies: some downplay their coauthors, while others using the plural "we" to appear unanimous or authoritative. These features are important for better understanding how Paul interjects or blends in with his coauthors, when coauthors have a clearer voice and might supplant Paul, and why orthonyms are activated at certain instances.

Rather than merely note that Paul co-wrote letters with enslaved and formerly enslaved literate workers (named and unnamed) and continue to interpret as though Paul is the singular Great Man behind these epistles, I want to use this final section to slow down and ask what might change if we move beyond this *solus Paulus* mentality. There are two subpoints I want to make here: (1) we ought to pay attention to moments where the letter-writer uses the first-person pronoun *and* an orthonym (e.g., "I, Paul"), and (2) we might consider if every use of "I" should automatically be assumed to have *Paul* behind it.

While Pauline+ epistles tend to use the first-person singular "I" quite a lot, not every use of "I" is followed by a name. There are nine instances across the Pauline+ epistles in which the writer attaches Paul's name to the pronoun, and

---

107 Pol. *Phil.* 3.2.

108 On the concept of a shifting "we-circle" (*Wir-Kreises*), see Heckel, "Die Historisierung," 433–434.

109 Pol. *Phil.* 13.2.   110 Burini, *Lettera*, 63–64; Hartog, *Polycarp*, 47–53, 97.

I want to take a moment to examine what work the name of Paul does. Perhaps the most obvious cases are those in which Paul attaches his name to the letter to highlight his own authorial presence at the end of two letters: 1 Corinthians and Philemon. It was not uncommon for Greek and Roman authors to utilize (formerly) enslaved literate labor to produce a majority of the letter themselves before adding some smaller portion in their own hand, often to confirm one's position as author (via dictation to a literary worker), to boost one's authority among its readers, or to compensate for one's physical absence among the recipients.[111] While scholars often focused on the features of Paul's autograph and its large letters – particularly in Galatians[112] – I want to focus on the additional use of Paul's *name* in 1 Corinthians and Philemon. It is notable that in his monoauthored letter to the Galatians, Paul merely uses the first-person pronoun without clarifying who he was: "See with what large letters I wrote to you in my hand" (6:11). By contrast, Paul adds his name to 1 Corinthians and Philemon, two letters that he coauthors with Sosthenes and Timothy, respectively:

> "The greeting in my hand – [of] Paul" (1 Cor 16:21)
> "I, Paul, wrote in my own hand." (Phlm 19)

While Paul adds his autograph elsewhere for a variety of reasons, he only explicitly attaches his orthonym in this manner to some coauthored letters. This suggests that Paul is aware that there might be some ambiguity surrounding the authorial "I" when addressing the reader. In the case of 1 Corinthians 16, Paul likely interrupts his enslaved literate worker to add his name as a signature – and, notably, Sosthenes does not take the same space to do so. Likewise in Philemon, Paul's authorial presence mostly drowns out Timothy, with only one use of "we" (Phlm 6), which likely refers to Paul and the epistle's recipients rather than exclusively to Paul and Timothy. And yet, Paul steps in once more with a joint autograph and orthonym to convince Philemon (somewhat tongue-in-cheek) that he will personally pay back any debts for Onesimus's purported wrongdoings (Phlm 19, 21).[113]

Pseudo-Pauline texts pick up on this deployment of Paul's onymity. 2 Thessalonians 3:17 protests too much by producing an autograph, Paul's name, *and* a claim that every one of Paul's letters have both of these features. Despite this claim being easily disproven, the writer(s) of 2 Thessalonians

---

[111] Reece, *Paul's Large Letters*, 51–69; Moss, "Secretary."

[112] Fewster, "Can I Have Your Autograph?" 34–35.

[113] On Paul's deployment of *auctoritas* in Philemon, see Brookins, "I Rather Appeal." I would add that Paul's use of his own name functions as another deployment of *auctoritas* – here, in the sense of claimed authorship of a text that urges particular actions from Philemon.

recognizes that Paul's onymity does a particular type of work in connecting the author to the letter's recipients and shining a spotlight on one of the coauthors. At the same time, some translators do not always recognize or make explicit this treatment of coauthorship. Often the phrase Παύλου, ὅ ἐστιν σημεῖον ἐν πάσῃ ἐπιστολῇ (translated very woodenly, "of Paul, which is a sign in every letter") has additional pronouns added to it:

> "This is the mark of every letter *of mine*." (NRSV)
> "Which is the distinguishing mark in all *my* letters." (NIV)
> "This is the sign of genuineness in every letter *of mine*." (ESV)
> "I do this in all *my* letters to prove they are *from me*." (NLT)

The additional "my/mine/me" in such translations add something that the Thessalonian (pseudo-co-)authors are careful not to do: they make Paul the sole author of the epistle by making it *his* letter. While 2 Thessalonians spotlights Paul in an attempt to conform to Paul's use of his name elsewhere in his correspondence, it simultaneously recognizes that Paul tends toward valuing coauthorship and does not claim coauthored letters as his alone.[114] In fact, the only time any Pauline+ epistle attaches a pronoun to the word ἐπιστολή is in 2 Thessalonians itself, which was added out of concern that the Thessalonians will be fearful "because of a letter as if *from us*" (2 Thess 2:2) and urged them to stay strong in the teaching the three of them provided "either through word or through *our* letter" (2 Thess 2:15). Even recent work, which argues that the phrase "as if from us" (2 Thess 2:2) refers to the distinction between teachings *from Paul* and *from not-Paul* (e.g., a letter, a word, a spirit), still assumes that the "us" refers solely to Paul.[115] Unlike some translators who slip back into treating Paul as the Great Man behind each epistle, potential pseudepigraphs like 2 Thessalonians are more cautious about their portrayal of coauthorship.

Other explanations for the plural authorship of pseudo-Pauline letters have been offered. For example, Michael Goulder has suggested that the in-sync "we" (Paul and Silvanus) of 2 Thessalonians is presented as an attempt to fix Silvanus's failures at Thessalonica after being left there to clarify the message of 1 Thessalonians.[116] He goes so far as to argue that the "letter as if from us" (2.2) may not be a Pauline forgery, but a letter written by Silvanus in the names of

---

[114] Cf. 1 Cor 5:9–11, where Paul refers to previously having written about sexual immorality to the Corinthians "in the letter" (ἔγραψα ὑμῖν ἐν τῇ ἐπιστολῇ) and is now "writing to you" again (ἔγραψα ὑμῖν). Paul does not refer to the letter predating 1 Cor as exclusively his own, nor does he claim it in 1 Cor. The same goes for 2 Cor 10:9–11 regarding the "weighty and strong letters," which are not specified to be Paul's alone but are simply "the letters" (αἱ ἐπιστολαί) contrasted with Paul's weak body. Likewise, see treatments of 2 Pet 3:16 as "his [i.e., Paul's] letters."

[115] Brookins, "The Alleged 'Letter'."

[116] Goulder, "Silas," esp. 101–104. As a (formerly) enslaved literate worker, Silvanus may have been tasked by Paul with reading or interpreting the letter after its composition.

himself, Paul, and Timothy to the Thessalonians.[117] The heightened use of the Pauline orthonym as a marker of Paul's presence may be read as a consequence of the writer(s) of 2 Thessalonian's concern about the dangers of coauthorship. That is to say, coauthored letters have the ability to make multiple writers appear as though they speak in unison on particular issues, but also makes possible misrepresentations of one's positions. 2 Thessalonians may have used Paul the Great Man to delimit acceptable coauthored texts by claiming that the only "we" who the Thessalonians should listen to are the "we" that center on and conform to Paul's voice and thoughts.

As noted earlier, there is a shift in Pauline studies toward recognizing that coauthors may have had a more substantial impact on the production of what we have traditionally called "Pauline" thought or language than previously considered.[118] Seeking out coauthorial impact challenges a long history of considering Paul as the "Great Man" behind letters like 1 Corinthians.[119] Often, attempts to uncover the words or thoughts of Paul's coauthors takes one of two directions. The first is that coauthors are represented in the first-person plural "we" of the text – Paul *et cetera*. Paul stands at the center of such a model, with others circulating around the Great Man and being called upon when deemed necessary (if ever necessary?) for his line of argumentation. The second approach seeks out common language or motifs across Pauline epistles that might allow a glimpse of a coauthor's words. For example, Benjamin Sargent has suggested that shared language of sanctification in 1 Thessalonians and 1 Peter may point to Silvanus as the authorial voice behind certain sections of those epistles.[120]

What I would like to suggest is a third possibility for experimenting with the coauthorial voices of many Pauline epistles: What if not every "I" in the Pauline epistles is meant to be Paul? This suggestion challenges our deeply ingrained assumption that the Pauline epistles are *Paul's and no one else's*, that only Paul can truly speak through them, and that all other figures are merely supporting actors for the superstar (or superapostle). If we conclude that Paul is not alone in his epistolary production, then it is worth exploring how these coauthors may have actually made a difference to the text; if not, then we slip right back into treating them as "courtesy" authors. To experiment with this approach, I want to focus on the only portion in the Pauline+ epistles where Paul appears to be talking in the third-person: 1 Corinthians 1–3.

As noted earlier, 1 Corinthians is attributed to two authors (Paul and Sosthenes) and that Paul is careful to add his name in statements where he is

---

[117] Goulder, "Silas," 101.   [118] Moss, *God's Ghostwriters*, 77–79.

[119] Note how even early Christian literature within a generation or two of Paul (e.g., *1 Clement* 47.1–2) obscures 1 Corinthian's coauthorship by referring to Paul as its sole writer.

[120] Sargent, "Chosen through Sanctification."

concerned about ambiguity over his recipients identifying which "I" is speaking. I would suggest that this orthonymic move leaves open the interpretive possibility that, at least on some occasions, the "I" of a Pauline letter need not be Paul. 1 Corinthians 1 begins in the first-person singular, with the "I" thanking God for the Corinthians, exhorting them to avoid divisions, and quoting Chloe's people (likely part of her enslaved retinue) who reported quarrels: "Each of you say: 'I belong to Paul!' 'But I belong to Apollos! 'But I belong to Cephas!' 'But I belong to Christ!'" (1:12). What interests me here is how the author of 1 Corinthians 1 goes on to speak about Paul in the third-person, noting that Christ wasn't divided, nor: "Was Paul crucified for you? Or were you baptized in the name of Paul?" (1:13). What might change if we read the reply to the message from Chloe's people as the words of Sosthenes rather than Paul? One substantial change would be that Sosthenes becomes responsible for baptizing Crispus, Gaius, and the household of Stephanas (1:15–16). Instead of viewing the statement "I thank God that I didn't baptize any of you" (1:14) as Paul's tongue-in-cheek gratefulness that his baptism of a few Corinthians did not exacerbate the production of factionalism, we could read this statement as Sosthenes's passive-aggressive relief that his name was not added to the list of Corinthian divided loyalties.[121]

The authorial figure goes on to claim that Christ did not send him to baptize, but to preach the gospel "and not with eloquent wisdom" (1:17). While it is possible to read this passage as Paul's, given that Paul is deeply concerned with the mismatch between his epistolary words and physical presence in 2 Corinthians, this need not be the case. Murphy-O'Connor has pointed to 1 Corinthians 1:18–31, which focuses on the paradoxical relationship between wisdom and foolishness among Jews, Greeks, Jesus-adherents, and God, as a coauthored concept between Sosthenes and Paul. He notes that Gordon Fee reads 1 Corinthians 1:23 – the famous "we proclaim Christ crucified" – as Paul's rhetorical attempt to claim that others besides himself are as invested in Jesus's crucifixion as the crux of salvation history.[122] In response, Murphy-O'Connor argues that "the nature of Paul's evocation of all believers through the use of 'we' [. . .] is markedly different to what appears here, and there is reason to think that Paul was in fact unique in his consistent stress on the brutal modality of Christ's death."[123] This leaves open the possibility for us to foreground Sosthenes as the main speaker and Paul as the secondary figure in the "we" of

---

[121] See Concannon, *Assembling Early Christianity*, 190–191, 200–208; and Eusebius, *Hist. eccl.* 2.25.8, on contested claims regarding which figures founded the Corinthian assembly.

[122] Fee, *First Epistle*, 75n34. Barrett, *The First Epistle*, 54 also includes the audience in the "we" of 1 Cor 1:23.

[123] Murphy-O'Connor, "Co-authorship," 568.

1 Corinthians 1:23. In this reading, Christ sends Sosthenes to proclaim the gospel and its apparent foolishness and weakness in a world still caught up in human wisdom and strength.

Similarly, Murphy-O'Connor has suggested to read 1 Corinthians 2:6–16 as a coauthored section by both Paul and Sosthenes focused on how "we" speak God's secret wisdom inaccessible to this age's rulers, which were revealed to "us" through God's spirit. He specifically counters the interpretations of E. E. Ellis, who suggests Paul incorporated an argument produced by a Pauline pneumatic group, as well as Gordon Fee, who treats the plural as functionally equivalent to the singular "I" despite the lack of evidence that Paul typically speaks in the plural about himself.[124] Rather, Murphy-O'Connor notes a shared pattern between 1 Corinthians 1:16–31 and 2:6–16: two citations from Jewish scripture with exposition sandwiched in between that contain "we" statements. This leads him to suggest that Sosthenes is the main figure behind both passages, as someone who intimately knew the Corinthian *ekklēsia* – and that "Paul took the advice of a collaborator as regard form and content, which gave the latter the status of a co-author."[125] However, he reads both 1 Corinthians 2:1–5 and 3:1–4 as an irritated Paul interrupting his coauthor with "and I!" (κἀγώ; 2:1 and 3:1).

But does the preceding section written in the first-person (1 Cor 2:1–5) need to be read as Paul's interruption, sandwiched between two coauthored statements that highlight Sosthenes's knowledge of the Corinthians? Following on the coattails of 1:16–31, the "I" of 2:1–5 still focuses on types of wisdom and knowledge via the spirit. Reading this passage instead as the words of Sosthenes, Sosthenes again highlights how he comes to the Corinthians "not with excellent speech or wisdom" (2:4), mirroring his statement in 1:17, as well as that "I decided" (2:2) to know Christ crucified, mirroring his claim that "we" made in 1:23. Sosthenes becomes a figure who was with the Corinthians without strong speech that appeared wise to many in the community, but with "a demonstration of the spirit and power" (2:4). The transition from language of wisdom and weakness in Section 1 to language of wisdom and spirit in Section 2 suggests that – unlike Ellis – we do not need to read 2:6–16 as replicating or mocking a pneumatic Corinthian group's claims. The argument in 2:6–16 matches what "we" (Sosthenes and Paul) are doing in Corinth: speaking through God's wisdom which is both revealed through God's spirit and is incomprehensible to many in this world. We can still find jabs against Corinthian opponents in the phrasing of the "psychical person" (2:14), but the line of argumentation and conception of the spirit as a provider of God's wisdom fits Sosthenes and Paul's own claims.

---

[124] Ellis, *Prophecy*, 26; Fee, *First Epistle*, 101n13; Murphy-O'Connor, "Co-authorship," 567–570.
[125] Murphy-O'Connor, "Co-authorship," 569–570.

I have argued that coauthorship in the Pauline+ repertoire is something that we might take more seriously as we explore *how* Paul and the constellation of (formerly) enslaved literary workers write. Why are the names of coauthors attached to many of these letters, rather than just a more ambiguous "we"? What is gained by attaching the names of Sosthenes, Silvanus, and Timothy for the epistles' readership?

I want to conclude with two points. First, the Pauline+ repertoire's use of Paul's name suggests that orthonyms function quite similarly to pseudonyms. "Paul" is evoked in order to persuade readers to buy into the image of Paul's apostolic authority that he and later writers found so powerful, to provide texts with a stamp of approval, and to differentiate the Pauline voice from coauthors in order to offer a personal or pointed note. What is significant here is that author function is not necessarily that different between Paul's own use of his name in "genuine" epistles and others' uses of Paul's name in "forged" epistles. In both cases, the onymic act does similar types of work for its writers; *we* are the ones who often classify them as distinct authorial acts based on our historical-critical or theological impulses to differentiate the words of the "historical Paul" from other Pauls and from the enslaved and formerly enslaved workers who made possible Paul's epistolary habits.

Second, future scholarship in Pauline studies might continue toward a growing awareness of *coauthor function* and further explore how Timothy, Silvanus, and Sosthenes (as well as many other enslaved and formerly enslaved literate workers) played a role in the production, composition, and/or deployment of authorial figures. It is easy to presume that Paul's coauthors play little role in his letters, but this assumption overlooks how ancient literature often works hard to obscure the plethora of people involved in the production of texts. To continue to skim past even coauthors – who are explicitly named in the Pauline+ repertoire – is to read along the grain too quickly and buy into Paul's rhetoric of his almost-singular importance among itinerant Jesus-adherent preachers. Paul worked within a web of people, a network of writers and thinkers and actors whose presence (visible or invisible, free or enslaved) deserves our attention.

3 Centos, Heresy, and the Authorial Order
of Christian Literature

How did the "correct" authorship of other writers' texts function as a claim that some early Christian writers could deploy and defend? While there are plenty of directions to approach this topic, my focus here falls on early Christian heresiology and cento poetry. Centos are a form of cut-and-paste poetry that rearranged lines from earlier authors and texts, and so often sat at the edge of authorial paradigms: they are both something belonging to the "original" author and to the "new" author. Their ambiguity troubled two early Christian writers in particular: Irenaeus of Lyons and Tertullian of Carthage, both of whom compare their opponents' approaches to scriptural interpretation to cento composition. Anxiety over the teachings and biblical interpretations of "heretics" provides us with an opportunity to explore the limits of orthonymity and authorial attribution. When does a text no longer "belong to" the person who wrote it? At what point does the "author's intention" matter or not, according to Irenaeus and Tertullian?

My argument consists of three parts. After an introduction to cento poetry in (late) antiquity, I will turn to Irenaeus's comparison between heretical scriptural interpretation and cento production to explore what limits there are (or are not) for understanding the "authorial intention" of the Gospel of John. Then, I will turn to Tertullian's cento-heretical hermeneutic comparison. With Tertullian, I focus on his rhetoric of ignorance and attribution, in which he suggests that a purported orthonym like "Vergil" or "Homer" ought not be applied if a text is changed too much. While Irenaeus and Tertullian have different limits to the application of the orthonym to cento poetry and scripture, their concern lets us see how they envision authorial attributions being applied to or removed from texts. With too many changes to vocabulary, style, or order, the name attached to a text may no longer be "properly" represented or interpreted in the eyes of some early Christian writers.

Centos are a form of late ancient poetry in which a writer takes lines and half-lines from formerly written texts and arranges them to produce a new narrative. The term refers to patchwork garments, since they are stitched together from various snippets of literature.[126] Since Vergil and Homer were the two authors most commonly dismembered for cento poetry, such poetic recompositions were usually in dactylic hexameter. Until recent decades, cento poetry was often denigrated in classical scholarship as a cheap knock-off of the most prominent canonical authors.[127] However, scholars have gained interest in cento poetry both for its capacity to help us understand the reception of Vergilian and Homeric literature in late antiquity, as well as how it makes accessible writings by elite women like Faltonia Betitia Proba (fourth century) and the empress Aelia Eudocia (ca. 401–460).[128] While the practice likely emerged in Hellenistic Alexandria,[129] it became prominent in the fourth to sixth centuries CE and is best-preserved in Latin examples. Additionally, as

---

[126] Hardie, *Classicism and Christianity*, 21.

[127] Bailey, *Anthologia Latina*, iii, who calls the genre a "disgrace to literature" (*opprobia litterarum*).

[128] McGill, *Vergil Recompose*; Sowers, *In Her Own Words*; Lefteratou, *The Homeric Centos*.

[129] Pollmann, "Sex and Salvation," 59–60.

Irene Peirano Garrison has examined in depth, Vergil became a popular text in late antiquity to mine "for illustrations of different rhetorical principles."[130] Late ancient writers took interest in re-reading and re-crafting earlier literature to make rhetorical and theological points. For example, some near-contemporaneous Christian texts, like Minucius Felix's *Octavius*, used centos to prove that non-Christians already had Christian concepts of God and Jesus hidden away in their own writings.[131] Others, like Irenaeus and Tertullian, treated centos as a threat because of the possibility of centonic polyvalence bleeding into scriptural interpretation. As William Johnson argues in his analysis of elite Roman reading communities, "the sometimes extensive excerpting of thoughtfully chosen texts served as a means of gaining control over these texts, often in conjunction with close study and memorizing, as a means of inculcating the reading certain essential masteries: of language of style [. . .] of ways of thought, of morals and character, of identity."[132] Early Christians were no exception as they re-tooled the textual material of others to control, delimit, or otherwise expand their hermeneutical affordances.

Two fourth-century centos highlight how centos challenged traditional boundaries of textual coherence and authorship. In 374 CE, Decimus Magnus Ausonius, an orator and teacher from Aquitaine, was challenged by the emperor Valentinian I to produce a wedding cento. In response, Ausonius wrote a raunchy Vergilian cento for the wedding of Valentinian's co-emperor and son, Gratian.[133] Ausonius's poem describes the bride and groom, banquet, bedchamber, and the groom's rape of the bride on their wedding night in Vergil's recycled words. Ausonius blames the scene of sexual assault both on his readers and on Vergil himself for allowing such a scene to be stitched together, and consequently modern scholars have distanced Ausonius's cento from the purported "purity" of Vergilian literature.[134]

Scholarly distancing of Vergil from Ausonius's reuse sets the stage for my examination of how Irenaeus and Tertullian deal with the problem of *authorial intent*. Writers and scholars look back on cento poetry's source material and often ask whether the "original" author meant for their text to be read as the centoist arranged it, or whether the centoist brings their own bias into the textual arrangement. Ausonius preempts accusations that he purposefully misconstrues Vergil's words, for example, by arguing that Vergil should not have produced

---

¹³⁰ Peirano Garrison, *Persuasion*, 222. See also Peirano Garrison, *The Rhetoric*, 74–116 on late ancient pseudepigraphic biographies of Vergil, as well as the extensive expansion of Vergil's textual repertoire through authorial attribution after his death.

¹³¹ Minucius Felix, *Oct.* 19.1–2 and its use of the *Aeneid* and *Georgics*.

¹³² Johnson, *Readers*, 201.

¹³³ For the Latin text and commentary of Ausonius's *Cento nuptialis*, see Green, *Ausonii*, 145–158.

¹³⁴ Cullhed, "In Bed with Virgil."

textual material that could be misconstrued in the first place. For both ancient (elite male) readers and modern (mostly male) scholars of Ausonius's cento, the problem has traditionally not been the act of rape itself, but the way that *Vergil's name* is attached to and implicated in sexual violence. How "Vergilian" a Vergilian cento like the *Cento nuptialis* (*Wedding Cento*) is has mattered for those invested in salvaging Vergil and other authors from illicit ideas or practices.

Perhaps most important for my purposes is Ausonius's prefatory letter to the cento written to Axius Paulus, where he takes particular interest in the composition and function(s) of centos. He describes centos as a type of "compilation" (*concinnatio*), as well as a "collection of fragments and an integration of lacerated pieces" (*sparsa college et integrare lacerata*), highlighting the piecemeal, cut-and-paste nature of cento composition.[135] Along with explaining how centos hexameters are produced, Ausonius conceptualizes the poetic outcome as a "continuum from disjointed parts, one from diverse parts, ludicrous from serious parts, mine from another's (*de inconexis continuum, de diversis unum, de series ludicrum, de alieno nostrum*).[136] He finds his text to be something frivolous (*frivolum*) and comparable to a game (*ludo*; *ludicro*), even comparing it to a Greek game called *stomachion* in which bone pieces are (re)arranged into different images.[137] The Christian heresiologist Irenaeus, discussed more below, uses a similar image to critique his opponents by claiming that their heretical scriptural interpretation is comparable to the rearrangement of a mosaic that depicts a king into that of a fox.[138] Irenaeus was deeply concerned with making sense of the diversity of pluriform gospel textuality, and – like many of his second-century Christian counterparts – devised hermeneutical approaches and boundaries to make sense of how diverse or unified particular narratives or texts might be.[139]

Ausonius's theorizing of cento composition is not only important for laying out the relationship between diversity and unity, but also for his understanding of cento authorship. He presents the *Cento nuptialis* as "ours" (*nostrum*) built out of the discombobulated components of something that is "foreign" or "belonging to another" (*de alieno*). Ausonius's cento asserts to have his name rightly attached to it, despite its Vergilian source material. As Jaś Elsner put it,

---

[135] Ausonius, *Cento nuptialis*, pref. 4–5 (Green, *Ausonii*, 146).

[136] Ausonius, *Cento nuptialis*, pref. 25–26 (Green, *Ausonii*, 146).

[137] Ausonius, *Cento nuptialis*, pref. 1, 13, 39–52 (Green, *Ausonii*, 145–147).

[138] Irenaeus, *Haer.* 1.8.1.

[139] See esp. Coogan and Rodriguez, "Ordering Gospel Textuality"; Coogan, "Meddling with the Gospel." The sociohistorical realities of non-linear reading and rearrangement of textual material (see Coogan, "Gospel as Recipe Book") were both deployed by early Christian heresiologists in their own textual hermeneutic and challenged by them as beyond the pale.

Ausonius focuses heavily on literary play, the puzzlement of unity and disunity, and "the claim of ownership despite the overt plagiarism."[140] However, it is unclear whether Ausonius's contemporaries would understand the writing of centos to function like our modern concept of plagiarism. Classical scholarship has demonstrated that advanced students of Greek and Latin literature often learned to parrot the vocabulary and style of prominent writers (especially Homer and Vergil) through *imitatio, prosopopoeia,* and declamations.[141] The capacity for utilizing random lines of prominent texts or rearranging them was also popular in late antiquity in the form of sortilege and bibliomancy. For example, some Greek magical papyri assigned dice roll numbers to Homeric verses as a form of divination, and late ancient Christians used gospel manuscripts opened at random to predict future events or answer questions.[142] While forms of sortilege and divination are certainly different than cento poetry, they deployed segmented textual material and raised similar questions for late antique (especially Christian) writers: could a text like the Gospel of John have a hidden or additional meaning beyond what they believed to be John's "authorial intention"?

Faltonia Betitia Proba, a contemporary of Ausonius, likewise produced a Vergilian cento that raises questions about authorial attribution and, for some late ancient writers, the dangers of women interpreting canonical material. In her *Cento Vergilianus de laudibus Christi* (*Vergilian Cento on the Glory of Christ*, ca. 360 CE), Proba produced a 694-hexameter Vergilian cento that explored creation, the fall and flood, and Jesus's restitution of the world.[143] While Proba does not offer the same type of prefatory theorization of the cento as Ausonius, her assertions about the Vergilian cento and the rebuttals of near-contemporaries reveal varied perspectives on the relationship between the *hypotext* (e.g., Vergil) and the *hypertext* (e.g., Proba's cento).[144] Proba presents herself as "the prophetess Proba" (*vatis Proba*) who is producing a "sacred song" (*sacrum … carmen*) for God through the indwelling Holy Spirit; she claims the song as her own, but also that "I will indicate that Vergil sang the holy gifts of Christ" (*Vergilium cecinisse loquar pia munera Christi*).[145] In her recollection or repetition (*repetens*) of Vergilian lines, Proba claims to unscramble a hidden Christian Vergil and bypass standard conceptions of "authorial intent" by demonstrating that even Vergil did not know his writings' purpose.

---

[140] Elsner, "Late Narcissus," 181.

[141] Peirano Garrison, *The Rhetoric*, 1–35; Cribiore, *Gymnastics*, 220–244.

[142] Maltomini, "P. Lond. 121"; Wisniewski, "Pagans, Jews, Christians."

[143] White, *Early Christian Latin Poets*, 39.   [144] McGill, "Virgil."

[145] Proba, *Cento Vergilianus* ll. 13, 18, 47–55, and 23, respectively (Clark and Hatch, *Golden Bough*, 16–21); McGill, "Virgil," 175–176.

Proba's role as orthonymous author of the cento does not dismiss her Vergilian source material, nor the capacity provided by God and the Spirit to produce the text.

Both a later scribe of Proba's *Cento* and Jerome interpreted Proba's cento otherwise. The scribe's preface accompanied a luxury manuscript for Theodosius II and Arcadius, claiming that Proba's work had "changed for the better Maro with divine meaning" (*Maronem mutatum in melius divino* [...] *sensu*).[146] The scribe implicitly dismisses Proba's claim that Vergil has some innate Christianness in his words that she prophetically uncovered, and instead proposes that Proba infused Vergil with a Christianness he lacked. From a different angle, one of Jerome's letters to Paulinus of Nola (394 CE) laments – much like Irenaeus and Tertullian below – that various people (especially women) have torn apart scriptural texts and used them in unacceptable ways. He attacks those who persuade fellow Christians that women are capable of teaching men and those who believe that their own scriptural interpretation is more reliable than written material passed down over generations. Jerome attacks those he thinks "do not deign to learn what the prophets and apostles thought," but who instead take "incongruent passages" (*incongrua* [...] *testimonia*) and shape them "to their own thought" (*ad sensum suum*) – thereby "depriving the intention" (*depravare sententias*) of scriptural texts.[147] Jerome then turns to the production of Homeric and Vergilian centos as a comparand, arguing that even though some cento writers find hints of Jesus's narrative or words in his texts, "we ought never call Christless Maro a Christian" (*non sic etiam Maronem sine Christo possimus dicere Christianum*).[148]

Along with attacking the female prophetic authority claimed by Proba,[149] Jerome differs from Proba in his understanding of authorial attribution and intent. He argues that scriptures are imbued with a certain *sententia* – an intention, view, or sense – by their apostolic authors that later cento writers (or women or heretical Christians) are attempting to bend to their own *sensus*. Proba, as both an *author* of a text who claims to extract Vergil's Christianness and as a *prophet/teacher*, interrupts Jerome's vision for Christianness only being extractable from Christian scriptures and from male leadership.[150] For Jerome, the purported orthonym *Vergil* signifies a non-Christian text that never was and never will be part of his Christian literary repertoire; for Proba, Vergil's authorial intentions did not preclude the possibility of finding a Vergilian Christ. In short, the debacle of authorship and (scriptural/Vergilian) hermeneutics

---

[146] Proba, *Cento Vergilianus* dedication ll. 4–5 (Clark and Hatch, *Golden Bough*, 12–13); McGill, "Virgil," 173–174.

[147] Jerome, *Ep.* 53.7.2. The Latin can be found in Hilberg, ed., *Hieronymi Epistulae*, 453–454.

[148] Jerome, *Ep.* 53.7.3.   [149] McGill, "Virgil," 177–180.   [150] Green, "Proba's Cento."

between Jerome and Proba represent a debate still ongoing for many scholars: do we uphold *authorial intent* or *reader response*? For whom is the "correct" reading what they believe the author's *sententia* to be, and what other interpretative and authorial possibilities are there?

Often, scholars treat the centoist as a plagiarist or forger rather than reading them in their own right.[151] Because of the prioritization of the classical or biblical texts as having a *sententia* that needs to be kept pure from centoists, how centoists (and their opponents) talk about the fragility of authorial attribution and intention is easily overlooked. How is a text labeled as Vergil's, Proba's, Ausonius's, John's, or multiple authorial figures at once – and how does that impact the possibility for a singular or diverse interpretation(s) of the text?

Irenaeus of Lyons's five-book *Against Heresies* (*Haer.*) offers both a description and a refutation, especially of teachings that he believes stem from Valentinus, a mid-second-century preacher in Rome whose influence and followers spread quickly across the Mediterranean. Much of Book 1 is dedicated to an exposition of what Irenaeus deems a common Valentinian mythological and etiological system about the creation of the world (*Haer.* 1.1–7), his refutation of their use of scriptural phrases and ideas (1.8–9), Irenaeus's concept of the universal unity of the church (1.10), and a long discussion of Valentinian and non-Valentinian "heretics" including Marcion, Tatian, Sethians, and Cainites (1.11–31).[152] We cannot take Irenaeus at his word regarding what Valentinians were writing, saying, and doing, especially since he purposefully and polemically links any people or groups of whom he disapproved into a heretical lineage.[153]

My focus falls primarily on *Haer.* 1.8–9, where Irenaeus ends his description of the Valentinian cosmological system and turns toward refutation of their scriptural repertoire and hermeneutics. He not only claims that Valentinian cosmology is constructed out of something unlike what the prophets, Jesus, or apostles ever wrote or said, but that "they select from sources that are not scriptures" (*de eis quae non sunt scriptura legentes*).[154] Irenaeus oscillates between two distinct claims: that Valentinians *have and pervert* authoritative texts shared with other Christians for their own advantage, and that they *use other* texts. He especially worries that his opponents "disregard the order and connection of the scriptures" (*ordinem quidem et textum scripturarum*

---

[151] Karanika, "Female Voice," 96.

[152] On the structure of *Haer.*, see Behr, *Irenaeus of Lyons*, 73–120.

[153] Pagels, "Irenaeus," 343–344; Robertson, "Polemic of Individualized Appellation."

[154] Irenaeus, *Haer.* 1.8.1. The Greek and Latin text of *Haer.* I use is from Rousseau and Doutreleau, *Irénée de Lyon, Livre I*; Rousseau and Doutreleau, *Irénée de Lyon, Livre III*.

supergradientes; τὴν μὲν τάξιν καὶ τὸν εἱρμὸν τῶν γραφῶν ὑπερβαίνοντες), "transferring and changing" passages (*transferunt autem et transfingunt*; μεταφέρουσι δὲ καὶ μεταπλάττουσι) and "making one thing out of another" (*et alterum ex altero facientes*; ἄλλο ἐξ ἄλλου ποιοῦντες) – a topic we will turn to next.[155] Valentinian scriptural interpretation, in Irenaeus's view, is similar to Jerome's concerns about scriptural interpretation among those he deems ignorant. In both cases, the *sensus* is altered to make a new point from material that Irenaeus and Jerome believe ought to be read in a different way. For Irenaeus, scriptural texts have particular "words, expressions, and parables" that have been properly arranged by prophets and apostles through God,[156] and so have a preset and plain reading that even heretics should follow.

This critique is most explicit in Irenaeus's Valentinian reading of John 1.[157] To begin, Irenaeus lays out how Valentinians purportedly find evidence for the existence of eight divine emanations (the Ogdoad) through John's gospel: the Forefather and Thought, Mind and Truth, Word and Life, and Human and Church.[158] He expresses frustration not only at this interpretation of John 1, but claims that:

> They teach that John, the disciple of the Lord, taught (*docent*; διδάσκουσι) the first Ogdoad, expressing themselves in these words: "John, the disciple of the Lord, wishing to speak about (βουλόμενος εἰπεῖν) the origin of all things, so as to explain how the Father produced the whole, lays down a certain principle ...[159]

For Irenaeus, a key issue of Valentinian interpretation of John is their claim that it was John's *authorial intent* to hide away subtle references to the Ogdoad in his prologue on the descent and incarnation of the Logos.[160] In order to claim that John's authorial intention is known and recoverable, Irenaeus aims to prove Valentinian interpreters "wholly wrong by this very gospel," both using John's own words against them and presuming that the gospel writer's words are passed down in a manner that maintains his intentions.[161] Irenaeus's argument requires that John remains the reliable and accessible *scriptor*, the author whose ideas and intention are retained. Valentinian exposition, according to Irenaeus,

---

155 Irenaeus, *Haer.* 1.8.1.

156 Irenaeus, *Haer.* 1.8.1: *sermones et dictiones et parabolas*; ῥήματα καὶ λέξεις καὶ παραβολὰς.

157 On Valentinian interest in John, see Pagels, *The Johannine Gospel*; Attridge, "Valentinians."

158 Irenaeus, *Haer.* 1.1.1.

159 Irenaeus, *Haer.* 1.8.5. The Latin text omits a portion of the Johannine commentary's claim that John "wished to speak" about origins.

160 See Harris, "Irenaeus's Engagement," 413–416, on how Irenaeus uses legal and rhetorical discourse to argue that readers need clearer evidence of John's authorial intentions than what Valentinians offer.

161 Irenaeus, *Haer.* 3.11.7.

threatened the integrity of John's authorial intention not only by excessively reading into the prologue for characters that are not there, but also by rearranging the textual material of John (and other texts) through their hermeneutical approach.

Irenaeus is not alone in arguing that authorial intent matters; in fact, his own opponents make the same literary and rhetorical moves. Ptolemy's *Letter to Flora* on the interpretation of Mosaic law uses the same types of arguments as Irenaeus regarding the "opinion" or "intention" (γνώμη) of Moses or God.[162] Just like how Irenaeus upholds the "oracles of the Lord" as the words that he fears heretics will corrupt, Ptolemy argues that proofs emerge "from the words of our savior."[163] Ptolemy offers three authorial figures for Mosaic law (God, Moses, and the elders) in order to explain what parts of Mosaic law Jesus challenges or upholds, and shares Irenaeus's concern that proper interpretation of scriptural passages involves being able to recognize authorial intent and authorial source. Irenaeus and Ptolemy share the assumption that there is a "correct" author whose *sensus* can be recovered and maintained through the correct assignment of authorship and intent.

While scholars have at times been quite interested in *Haer.* 1.8–9 and have examined it in light of ancient literary criticism, rhetorical theory, and the heresiological production of difference,[164] less time has been spent on Irenaeus's use of a Homeric cento as part of his anti-Valentinian literary and hermeneutical critique. Cento poetry plays a central role in Irenaeus's critique of the discombobulation of scripture that he attributes to Valentinians, as well as in establishing his "rule of truth" (*regula veritatis*) that becomes an Irenaean prerequisite for proper scriptural interpretation. Irenaeus picks up in *Haer.* 1.9 with his defense of Johannine exegesis, arguing that his opponents misuse John by asserting that it was "John's intention to exhibit that Ogdoad above."[165] Not only are figures like Human and Church lacking from John 1, Irenaeus notes, but such an interpretation also omits Jesus since he is not explicitly named in John's prologue.

This supposedly Valentinian practice of "collecting a set of expressions and names scattered around" (*dictiones et nomina dispersion posita colligentes*; λέξεις καὶ ὀνόματα σποράδον κείμενα συλλέγοντες) functions as the impetus for Irenaeus's discussion of cento poetry.[166] Irenaeus borrows from Pauline

---

[162] Ayres, "Irenaeus vs. the Valentinians," 166–167 on the *Letter to Flora*. Cf. Epiphanius, *Pan.* 33.4.7.

[163] Irenaeus, *Haer.* 1.8.1; Epiphanius, *Pan.* 33.3.8.

[164] Ayres, "Irenaeus vs. the Valentinians"; Harris, "Irenaeus's Engagement"; Pagels, "Irenaeus."

[165] Irenaeus, *Haer.* 1.9.1: *propositum esset Iohanni illam quae susum est Octonationem ostendere;* προέκειτο Ἰωάννῃ τὴν ἄνω Ὀγδοάδα μηνῦσαι.

[166] Irenaeus, *Haer.* 1.9.4.

vocabulary to claim that Valentinians twist scriptural texts "from being in accordance with nature to being contrary to nature" (*ex eo quote est secundum naturam in id quod est contra naturam*; ἐκ τοῦ κατὰ φύσιν εἰς τὸ παρὰ φύσιν). This practice of disassembling and reassembling textual is deemed comparable to Homeric centos, of which Irenaeus gives an example: from various lines of the *Iliad* and *Odyssey,* an unnamed writer produced a story about Heracles fighting Cerberus.[167]

> Having spoken, he sent me out, deeply groaning, from his house. (*Od.* 10.76)
> The hero Heracles, acquainted with great deeds. (*Od.* 21.26)
> Eurystheus, the son of Sthenelus, descended from Perseus. (*Il.* 19.123)
> To lead out the dog of wretched Hades from Erebus. (*Il.* 8.368)
> And he went forth like a mountain-bred lion, confident in his strength. (*Od.* 6.130)
> Swiftly through the city, and all his friends followed. (*Il.* 24.327)
> Maidens and youths and much-enduring old men. (*Od.* 11.38)
> Wailing miserably for him, as if he was going to his death. (*Il.* 24.328)
> But Hermes and the bright-eyed Athena sent him out. (*Od.* 11.626)
> For he knew in his heart how much his brother had to do. (*Il.* 2.409)

What interests me here is not the cento's content, but its framing within Irenaeus's argument about authorial intention and "correct" authorial attribution. Irenaeus worried that those he deemed "ignorant" (*idiotae*; ἀπειροτέρους) would believe that

> Homer actually composed the verses bearing upon that topic, which had in fact been newly constructed. Many others are snatched up by the sequential composition of the verses, so as to believe that Homer perhaps composed them.[168]

> *Ex temporali declamata controversia Homerum versus fecisse. Et multi abducantur per compositam consequentiam versuum, ne forte haec sic Homerus fecerit.*

> ἐπ᾽ ἐκείνης τῆς ἐξ ὑπογύου μεμελετημένης ὑποθέσεως Ὅμηρον τὰ ἔπη πεποιηκέναι, καὶ πολλοὺς συναρπάζεσθαι διὰ ταῦθ᾽ οὕτως Ὅμηρος εἴη πεποιηκώς.

The copy-and-paste style of the centos meant that the style of the hypotext (i.e., Homer) remained intact and was capable of convincing those who do not know their Homer well enough that the verses actually were Homer's. Irenaeus

---

[167] Irenaeus, *Haer.* 1.9.4. On this scene and its Homeric components, see Wilken, "Homeric Cento," 27–28. It is unclear whether Irenaeus himself composed this cento (Wilken, "Homeric Cento," 25–28) or whether he is citing an opponent's cento (Daniélou, *Message évangélique*, 2:73–101.

[168] Irenaeus, *Haer.* 1.9.4.

expected Christians to have a strong *paideia* to correctly identify both the *content* and *arrangement* of Homeric literature.[169] According to Irenaeus, the act of composition (*facio*; ποιέω) by an author draws the boundary regarding what possible textual affordances can remain latent or be activated within a given text.[170] Centos are a parallel to the threat of heretical scriptural interpretation because they expand the textual affordances allowable for interpreters: both involve scrambling terms and citations that sound right stylistically, but are rearranged to produce something that is (purportedly) distinct from the author's intention. As Karl Olav Sandnes notes, Irenaeus laments how the *verba* of texts can be manipulated to produce a new *sensus*. He compares Irenaeus's anxiety to second-history historiographical and literary concerns about textual "order" (τάξις), which was a common feature of early Christian management of pluriform gospel literature.[171] Pulling from Lucian's *How to Write History*, Diodorus Siculus's *Library of History*, and Dionysius of Halicarnassus's *Roman Antiquities*, Sandnes argues that Irenaeus is not alone in attempting to maintain a particular reading of textual material by advocating for controlling the *arrangement* of its passages.[172] For Irenaeus, an author's words are not completely stable on their own but are delimited by an author's textual arrangement. In the case of this cento, Homer's statements are only truly "Homeric" when arranged as (Irenaeus believes that) Homer intended.

Irenaeus is particularly concerned with how those who do not know Homer's compositional arrangement may be misled to believe the cento belongs to Homer's authorial voice – and, by extension, how those who do not know apostolic writers' compositional arrangements may fall prey to heretical textual rearrangements or authorial claims. For example, Irenaeus contrasts the "simple-minded man" (*simplicibus*; ἀπανούργων) with "one who is acquainted with Homeric topics" (*qui autem scit homerica*; ὁ δ᾽ ἔμπειρος τῆς Ὁμηρικῆς ὑποθέσεως ἐπιγνώσεται). The former is susceptible to believing the centoist's arrangement is how Homer "produced [the text] on this topic" (*in hoc argumento fecisse;* ἐπὶ ταύτης τῆς ὑποθέσεως πεποιηκέναι), whereas the latter will recognize that the verses are being applied to the wrong "subject" or "topic" (*argumentum*; ὑπόθεσιν).[173] The Homeric cento pulls from stories of Odysseus,

---

[169] Nevertheless, Irenaeus is also critical of Greek education as discombobulated and diverse (Grant, *Irenaeus*, 41–45).

[170] On affordances, see Levine, *Forms*, 6–9.

[171] See also Coogan and Rodriguez, "Ordering Gospel Textuality," 68–70, 82–84, on the centrality of τάξις to second-century treatment of the pluriform gospels.

[172] Sandnes, "The Rule of Faith," 5–8. In his condemnation of Tatian (*Haer.* 1.28.1), Irenaeus does not mention the *Diatessaron*, suggesting that Irenaeus either did not find it problematic or did not yet know about it, and thus could not object to its arrangement of textual material.

[173] Irenaeus, *Haer.* 1.9.4.

Heracles, Priam, Menelaus, and Agamemnon in order to produce its narrative of Heracles and Cerberus – that is, Homer's narratives are redeployed around new topics and subjects.

Irenaeus worried that his Valentinian opponents did the same thing with the Gospel of John, producing new narratives about figures like the Forefather and Achamoth out of verses that John (as Irenaeus claims) intended to be about Jesus. He argued that being able to return lines to their "proper location" (τῇ ἰδίᾳ) is comparable to what he hopes the rule of truth (*regulam veritatis*) can achieve – a educated and teachable recognition of when phrases are taken out of what Irenaeus deems their original context.[174] Only the "foolish" or "unlearned" fail to perceive this rule of truth and thus fail to recognize the dual pillars of *content* and *arrangement*.[175] Just as the classically educated recognize when a cento is not properly framed by Homer-as-author, those with access to the *regula veritatis* are deemed educated in a Christian sense to distinguish apostolic authorial writings from the "figment of these heretics."[176]

Irenaeus's "rule of truth" and its ability to determine "correct" textual and authorial arrangements emerges only through participation in what he deems proper reading communities.[177] That is to say, education about the "correct" authorship of apostolic writings through *content* and *arrangement* is something that occurs in communities that are tied to one another through the sharing of space and reading of literature. The arrangement of apostolic texts and phrases is something which Irenaeus claims that the unified and universal church passed down "harmoniously" (*consonanter*/συμφώνως) throughout the congregations of the Roman imperial world.[178] By the fourth century, as Jeremiah Coogan demonstrates, Christian use of textual technologies like tables and section divisions allowed for new means of delimiting the arrangement, content, and interpretation of gospel literature that Irenaeus sought to enforce years earlier.[179]

Irenaeus deemed the proliferation of texts and authors by Valentinians a problem during his exposition on the fourfold gospel, noting how they "offered their own compositions" (*suas conscriptiones proferentes*; ἴδια συγγράμματα ἐκφέροντες) and argued for more than four gospel texts.[180] Texts like the *Gospel of Truth* were deemed dangerous not only because they

---

[174] Irenaeus, *Haer.* 1.9.4; cf. Sandnes, *The Gospel*, 132–133. The Latin text does not mention returning to a "proper" location but rather to "its book" (*suo libro*).

[175] E.g., Irenaeus, *Haer.* 1.9.3; 3.11.9.   [176] Irenaeus, *Haer.* 1.9.4.

[177] On Irenaeus's pedagogical ideals, see Bingham, "Paideia and Polemic"; Ferguson, "Irenaeus." On education and delineation of textual meaning through communal reading practices, see Johnson, *Readers*, 9–16, 42–62; Cribiore, *Gymnastics*, 189–219.

[178] Irenaeus, *Haer.* 1.10.2. Cf. Pagels, "Irenaeus," 363–364.   [179] Coogan, *Eusebius*.

[180] Irenaeus, *Haer.* 3.11.9. See Coogan, "Meddling," 405–407, on the second-century obsession with "owning numerous books on the same subject" by Roman intelligentsia and its potential effects on discussions of pluriform gospel textuality.

claim to represent the truth that Irenaeus maintains only exists in his own rule of truth, but because any gospel-like text beyond the four gospels are deemed texts not "handed down from the apostles to us" (*quae ab apostolis nobis tradita sunt*; τὸ ὑπὸ τῶν ἀποστόλων παραδεδομένον) – as authored and published by another, even if heavily building upon apostolic textual material. Irenaeus is deeply invested in the idea that his *regula vertitatis* produces a clear (φανερός) and manifest (*manifestum*) reading of scripture, dependent upon the form (ἰδέα) of gospel texts: the "good composition and fitting together of pages" (*bene compositam e bene compaginatam*) of the "form of the gospels" (*speciem Evangelii*) that mirror God's own composition (*compositam*) of creation.[181] Proper composition and arrangement are baked into the structure of the cosmos and correctly display the divine content of the gospel texts, and so Irenaeus expects that scriptural authors and interpreters will honor that cosmological, theological, and bibliographic reality. The rule of truth functions as the scaffolding upon which Irenaeus hopes that Christian hermeneutics will be built, because the rule is capable of delimiting what arrangements of scriptural material and authorial attribution are deemed appropriate, as well as how far one can rearrange passages before the text becomes the material of a new (non-apostolic) author. The orthonymity and authorial intent of both the gospel writers and Homer are treated by Irenaeus as something only accessible when both textual and cosmological order are preserved.

Like Irenaeus, Tertullian saw cento poetry as exemplary of his own anxieties about threats to apostolic orthonymity, authorial intent, and the fungibility of textual material. Tertullian wrote *On the Prescription of Heretics* (*Praescr.*) around 203 CE to urge North African Christians to move beyond mere recognition of heresies and, like a fever that weakens the body, begin to eliminate those ideas by condemning those who purportedly weakened the community.[182] Tertullian suggested that Paul predicted the inevitability of heretics and factions among Christ-followers (e.g., 1 Cor 11:19), and thus that Christians had the capability to (mis)interpret scriptural texts. Tertullian understood those whom he deemed orthodox Christians to be in a difficult position, since they had to acknowledge both that heretics *needed* to exist but also find ways to deny heretics the right to appeal to scripture. This problem is often explained in *Praes.* as one of rightful possession of scripture:

> Therefore, we obstruct this to the highest degree by not admitting them to any discussion of the scriptures (*de scripturis disputationem*) at all. If the scriptures are their sources of strength, then the question ought to be sought out as

---

[181] Ayres, "Irenaeus," 169–180, esp. 176–177; Coogan, "Reading"; cf. Irenaeus, *Haer.* 3.11.9.

[182] Tertulllian, *Praescr.* 1–3. I follow the dating of Barnes, *Tertullian*, 55.

> to who is capable to be possessors of the scriptures (*possessio scripturarum*),
> so as not to admit their use by one who is not in any way capable [of
> possessing and interpreting them].[183]

Tertullian asked "who holds this faith, to which the scriptures belong?" (*quibus competat fides ipse, cuius sunt scripturae*), expecting that the answer is only those whom he deems Christians. He went so far as to claim that the "truth of scripture and interpretation and all Christian traditions" belongs firmly in the hands of his group, rather than that of heretics.[184] Ownership of not only texts, but also the hermeneutical ability to correctly read texts, is something that Tertullian aims to control and (re)claim for those he deems as having upheld the "rule of faith" (*regula fidei*).[185]

Tertullian took particular aim at what he deems an unnecessary and excessive quest for knowledge among his opponents – a "seek and you shall find" mentality he believes ended after Jesus's ascension.[186] Part of what he considered inappropriate knowledge-seeking included rejection of scriptural texts, rearrangement or excessive selectivity of scriptural passages, and the claim that the apostles withheld information about Jesus.[187] Even more so than Irenaeus, Tertullian worried about both a perceived "unfaithful meaning" (*adulter sensus*) and textual corruption by the likes of Valentinus and Marcion.[188] In arguing against other hermeneutical approaches, Tertullian suggested that correct scriptural interpretations have always belonged to his camp of Christians since they maintain an apostolic genealogy – leaving nothing but later invention, doctrinal diversity, or consciously wrong "choice" (*electione*) for heretics.[189]

This concern over doctrinal diversity and the "adulteration of scripture and interpretation" (*scripturam et expositionum adulteratio*; 38.1) leads us to Tertullian's use of centos and author function. Tertullian argued that, because scriptures rightly belong to those he deemed orthodox, heretics could not simply read scripture with its correct *content* and *arrangement* (because, if they did, they would be orthodox too!). Rather, heretical hermeneutics were only possible if either the content or arrangement were changed: "teaching differently" (*aliter docendi*) occurred through "arranging the doctrinal instruments differently" (*aliter disponendi instrumenta doctrinae*).[190] For Tertullian, Christian teaching

---

[183] Tertullian, *Praescr.* 15.3–4. Latin text from Refoulé, *Traité.*

[184] Tertullian, *Praescr.* 19.2, 19.3, respectively.

[185] For an overview, see Countryman, "Tertullian."

[186] E.g., Tertullian, *Praescr.* 8.2, critiquing his opponents' use of Matt 7:7 (par Luke 11:9).

[187] See esp. Tertullian, *Praescr.* 17 and 22–25. Cf. Sandnes, *The Gospel*, 12.

[188] Tertullian, *Praescr.* 17.2.   [189] Tertullian, *Praescr.* 37.2, 37.7.

[190] Tertullian, *Praescr.* 38.2. As Sandnes notes ("The Rule," 130–131), Tertullian conveniently rejects the patching together of scriptural material by his opponents, but uses similar techniques to prove that some gospel events were patchworked prophecies from Jewish scripture (e.g., *Marc.* 4.13).

and the texts from which they are purportedly extracted are intertwined, making it impossible to teach otherwise without altering the texts – either by rejecting certain texts outright (e.g., Marcion) or so radically changing the "proper" interpretation so as to basically produce a new text (e.g., Valentinus). Tertullian found these discombobulations of "original" textual meaning and authorial intent among his heretical opponents to be comparable to cento writers. He pointed to Hosidius Geta, one of our earliest named centoists known for compiling a tragedy of the *Medea* from Vergilian hexameter.[191] Martha Malamud suggests that Tertullian's anxiety about Hosidius Geta stems from how "centos expose the multivalent nature of language, forcing the reader constantly to focus on the protean ability of words to change their meanings depending on context."[192] In his own words, Tertullian worried about how the "material are compiled for the verses, and the verses for the material" (*materia secundum versus et versibus secundum materiam concinnatis*).[193] Similarly to the division of *verba* and *sensus* that we saw Sandnes propose earlier and to Ausonius's treatment of centos as a compilation (*concinnatio*), Tertullian's anxiety stems from how both biblical and Vergilian textual passages can be placed in new arrangements, such that perceived authorial intent is altered despite containing the same content. Writers are limited by both the content and ideas that they want to produce (the *materia*) and the textual material they are pulling from (the *versus*). Tertullian intervenes by claiming that heretics and cento writers both go too far in their willingness to adapt a *versus* to their own heretical *materia*.

Tertullian mentions two other poetic arrangements that bother him along-side Geta's *Medea*: a Vergilian cento of the narrative of the *Tablet of Cebes* written by one of Tertullian's relatives, and a group of Homeric cento writers (*Homerocentones*) who Tertullian describes as:

> Those who from the poems of Homer patch together into one body their own works, like one who stitches together rags, and put together out of many scraps from here or there.[194]

> *Qui de carminibus Homeri propria opera more centonario ex multis hinc inde compositis in unum sarciunt corpus.*

Note how Tertullian portrays cento poetry through two main features: its patchwork quality in order to create the illusion of unity, and its new authorial attribution. The patchwork language mirrors Ausonius's claim two centuries

---

[191] On the relationship between the *Medea* preserved in the sixth-century Codex Salmasianus and the one known by Tertullian, see Lamacchia, *Hosidii Getae*, vii–xiii; McGill, "Tragic Vergil."
[192] Malamud, "Double, Double," 161–162.   [193] Tertullian, *Praescr.* 39.3.
[194] Tertullian, *Praescr.* 39.5.

later that centos are a "collection of fragments and an integration of lacerated pieces" (*sparsa college et integrare lacerata*).[195] Ausonius and Tertullian agree that authorial attribution shifts in cento writing. Just as Ausonius argued that his wedding cento as "mine from another's" (*de alieno nostrum*), Tertullian lamented how Homeric cento poets made "their own works" (*propria opera*) out of what he deemed to be clearly and obviously Homer's.[196] Both centoists and their early Christian opponents conceived of cento poetry as not only a rearrangement of earlier poetic material to make a new story, but a shift in authorship. Geta's *Medea*, Tertullian's relative's Vergilian *Tablet of Cebes,* and the Homerocentones are characterized as attributable to their centoists rather than to Vergil or Homer.

Such an authorial attribution allows Tertullian to critique Marcion, whom he claimed "openly and plainly used the knife, not the stylus, since he cut the scriptures to accomplish his argument" (*exerte et palam machaera, non stilo usus est, quoniam ad materiam suam caedem scripturarum confecit*), as well as bash Valentinus, whom he argued "did not invent scriptures to suit his argument, but argument to suit the scriptures" (*non ad materiam scripturas sed materiam ad scripturas excogitavit*).[197] Like Tertullian's distinction between *materia* and *versus* mentioned earlier, he produces a similar distinction between *materia* and *scriptura*. Marcion, like a centoist, is accused of physically cutting-and-pasting passages in order to fit a preconceived *materia* – a subject that Marcion had purportedly predetermined and shaped his choice of passage mutilation around. Valentinus is accused of not even writing his own distinct text but rather producing a new narrative that fits the "correct" arrangement of the scriptural text. Rephrased: Tertullian treated Marcion as a threat for keeping the same *content* but changing the *arrangement,* and Valentinus for changing the *content* but keeping the same *arrangement* through reinterpreting passages like John 1. Even in his comparison between centoists and heretics, Tertullian argued that his texts are superior to Homer and Vergil by arguing that "the divine writings are more fruitful for the opportunity of any kind of topic" (*fecundior divine litteratura ad facultatem cuiuscumque materiae*).[198] At stake for Tertullian is defining proper authorship through restricting variation of arrangement and of textual interpretation, such that deviations by so-called heretics are deemed comparable to poets who cobble together new works (and new authorial attribution) out of previous authoritative textual material.

While Homer and Vergil have a longer history of being prophetic and creative textual repositories from which educated writers could pull *verba* for new

---

[195] Ausonius, *Cento nuptialis*, pref. 4–5 (Green, *Ausonii*, 146).
[196] Ausonius, *Cento nuptialis*, pref. 25–26 (Green, *Ausonii*, 146); cf. Sandnes, "The Rule," 13–14.
[197] Tertullian, *Praescr.* 38.9–10. Cf. Tertullian, *Val.* 1.3.   [198] Tertullian, *Praescr.* 39.6.

narratives or arguments, scriptures are envisioned as offering even more opportunities for rearrangement and new argumentation – a blessing and a curse from Tertullian's perspective. Much like Irenaeus, Tertullian turns to the contemporary practice of cento poetry as an example that he expects his readers will be familiar with, so as to underscore the vulnerability of scripture to mutilation and the ease with which heretics produce newly authored material in order to "pass" as apostolically author-ized.

Orthonyms – especially when attached to others' works – were an important factor in how some early Christians developed their rhetorical, ideological, and interpretative arguments. In the case of heresiologists like Irenaeus and Tertullian, orthonymity and author function offered the possibility to delineate what types of texts, textual arrangements, ideas, and narratives could be deemed acceptable or unacceptable. While a fuller theorization of cento poetry did not develop until the fourth and fifth centuries CE, already in the late second and early third centuries Irenaeus and Tertullian considered such poetic creations to be dangerous because of their ability to disrupt stable authorial claims. To both early Christian heresiologists and later centoists, the cento is a new poetic product whose compiler can rightfully attach their name to the text and function as a sort of name-on-record, a responsible signature. This suggests that such writers conceptualized orthonymous authorship as dependent not necessarily or exclusively on unique *content*, but certainly on the unique *arrangement* of textual material. Authorial intent for Irenaeus and Tertullian is bound up in textual organization, leading both to conclude that the authorial name attached to textual material can change with the text's arrangement or hermeneutical framework.

In some ways, Irenaeus and Tertullian's anxiety over cento-like Christian interpretation should not be surprising given the relationship between textual fixity and fluidity in early Christianity. Texts like the Gospel of Mark are prime examples, as Matthew Larsen has demonstrated, of "unfinished texts, accidental publication, and postpublication revision" that allowed for the writers of Matthew and Luke rearrange Marcan textual material.[199] Gospel literature entitled *Mark, Matthew,* and *Luke* are distinct snapshots within a stream of early Christian textual transmission of Jesus stories, rather than a series of finalized and solidified works. While Irenaeus in particular is comfortable proposing a fourfold gospel arrangement as a way of containing and controlling diversity of apostolic texts within a unified textual and authorial repertoire, the gospel texts that he elevates are themselves the product of a series of textual revisions and (re)arrangements that eventually led second-century Christians to

---

[199] Larsen, *Gospels before the Book*, 59; cf. Larsen, "Accidental Publication."

attribute these texts to distinct authors. What Irenaeus and Tertullian do in *Against Heresies* and *Prescription* is attempt to put an end to the production of *new* textual arrangements, to stymie the attribution of authoritative literature to anyone other than the apostles, and to mock those whom they deem gullible or ignorant for believing that a centoist or heretic's text could ever truly belong to an authorial figure like Homer, Vergil, or John. The assignment of "correct" authors and "correct" textual arrangement works to put boundaries on hermeneutical possibilities, and depends heavily on presumptions regarding the possibility of recovering and staying true to an author's intent.

4 Apologetic Orthonyms: Jewish Authors, Hellenic Historians, and Christian Catechesis

This final section explores the function of extradiegetic orthonymity between Hellenistic Jewish writers and early Christian writers. I am interested in how and under what conditions most early Jewish writers that we deem "correctly" attributed (e.g., Artapanus, Eupolemus) are used and preserved in Eusebius of Caesarea's fourth-century *Gospel Preparation* (*Praep. ev.*). Most of these authors – occasionally called the "minor Jewish historians" or "Hellenistic Jewish historians" – are only transmitted to us in this fragmentary form through the writings of Josephus, Clement of Alexandria, and Eusebius. Much scholarship has focused on producing standalone textual editions of these authors or assessing the (un)reliability of their quotes as mediated through other Jewish and Christian writers.[200] Following a different vein of scholarship spearheaded by Sabrina Inowlocki's examination of Eusebius's apologetic citational technique regarding Jewish authors,[201] I want to explore not only *how* Eusebius cites Jewish authors but *for what reason(s) he names* Jewish authors. What is at stake for Eusebius in the *Preparation* in providing the names of some of the earliest "correctly" named Jewish authors we know, and how does the assignment of orthonymous authorial attribution further his argument?

I'll start with a brief overview of Eusebius's *Preparation* and one of his primary sources for Jewish authors, Alexander Polyhistor's *On the Jews* (Περὶ Ἰουδαίων). I will then turn more broadly to Mediterranean literature to contextualize how and for what reason(s) writers cited texts by name. Third, I will examine the *Preparation*'s depiction of Polyhistor to elucidate how he is added to Eusebius's arsenal of Hellenic writers who know about and praise Jewish figures. I will end by asking how name-dropping functions as part of Eusebius's

---

[200] Holladay, *Fragments, Volume I*; Holladay, *Fragments, Volume II*; Holladay, *Fragments, Volume III*.

[201] Inowlocki, *Eusebius*.

apologetic toolkit, both to convince newly converted Christians of their rightful place in Hellenic culture and to divert them from seeking out such information themselves. The extradiegetic attribution of texts about Jews, Jerusalem, and biblical interpretation to named authorial figures works to justify Eusebius's claim that gentiles have – and should continue to – care about Jewish texts and Jewish authors.

Because my focus is on how Eusebius (and Polyhistor) used the names of Hellenistic Jewish historians, I will not talk much about the content or scriptural interpretation of what they preserved.[202] Instead, my emphasis is on how they *frame* each of these writers in relation to their literary production, to Polyhistor, and to Eusebius's goals in the *Preparation*. I argue that our "minor Jewish historians" constitute an example of apologetic orthonymity. Rather than actively attempting to preserve their names and interpretations of Jewish history and literature for their own sake, the names of some of our earliest orthonymous Jewish writers are preserved solely for Christian apologetic purposes – as sources used by Polyhistor whose names are only deemed valuable inasmuch as they prove to Eusebius's audience that some Hellenic writers read (and cared) about Jews and Jewish biblical interpretation. The "minor Jewish historians" are there to be "thought with" and examined in light of their Hellenic readership, rather than as standalone authors to be grappled with.

Eusebius, bishop of Caesarea, was a prominent fourth-century Christian writer who wrote in various genres: textual criticism, history, apologetics, martyrology, and more.[203] While best known for writing the *Ecclesiastical History*,[204] Eusebius also produced a two-volume text collectively known as the *Gospel Demonstration* (*Dem. ev.*), of which the first volume is called the *Gospel Preparation* (*Praep. ev.*), likely composed between 312–314 or 320–322 CE.[205] The *Preparation* is characterized by Eusebius as a preface to the entirety of the *Demonstration*, dedicated to a fellow bishop Theodotus and produced to educate newly converted Christians. In particular, Eusebius recognized that fulfillment of prophecy from Jewish scriptures (which is the goal of the latter half of the *Demonstration*) may not initially be convincing to a non-Jewish audience. To situate Christians in the Mediterranean landscape against stereotypes of its "unreasoned faith and unexamined assent,"[206] Eusebius both lays out common arguments leveled against Christians and demonstrates that

---

[202] See Dhont, "Greek Education and Cultural Identity."

[203] See recently Coogan, *Eusebius* on the bishop's extensive influence over late ancient and modern gospel interpretation.

[204] On Eusebius's interest in authorship analysis in *Hist. eccl.*, see Wyrick, *Ascension*, 305–308.

[205] Inowlocki, *Eusebius*, 17.   [206] Eusebius, *Praep. ev.* 1.1.11.

Jewish history (and, by extension, supersessionist Christian participation in Jewish history) is well-known and respected among Hellenes.[207] Having demonstrated that Christian acceptance of Jewish scripture and prophetic fulfillment is not illogical, Eusebius aims to prove that Hellenes often accept – and even prefer – Jewish culture and philosophy to their own.

While Eusebius cites a range of writers, including Josephus and Porphyry, one Hellenic historian stands out in Book 9: Cornelius Alexander Polyhistor. Polyhistor was likely born in Miletus in Asia Minor in the late second century BCE, was enslaved during the First Mithridatic War (88–84 BCE), and was forcibly brought to Rome.[208] He was subsequently manumitted, made a Roman citizen, and became a prominent Roman historian and ethnographer in the late Republican period.[209] We know that Polyhistor was a prolific writer through the various citations and mentions of works attributed to him: *On the Egyptians, On Bithynia, On the Euxine Sea, On India, On the Italians, On Caria*, a text on Illyria, and many other paradoxographic, ethnographic, and poetic treatises.[210] In many of these fragmentary or lost works, Polyhistor produces ethnographic and historical accounts through the writings of earlier indigenous and nonnative authors. Most important here is Polyhistor's *On the Jews*,[211] in which he preserves some Hellenistic Jewish and Samaritan biblical history through the writings of earlier poets, historians, chronographers, and tragedians.

Modern scholars and Eusebius have very different interests when it comes to using Polyhistor's *On the Jews* for the material that it cites, and have different concerns for how Hellenistic Jewish authorship functions. Historians of early Judaism have been deeply concerned with whether or not Polyhistor's citations of Hellenistic Jewish authors have been preserved faithfully and accurately.[212] As Jewish texts written in a Greek milieu, emphasis has also fallen on how to read these authors alongside other Greek-writing Jews (e.g., Philo; Josephus) and New Testament literature to contextualize their treatment of biblical narrative and history.[213] Individual studies have explored the diversity and contours of Hellenistic Greek writing and these various historians' and poets' contributions to that literary landscape.[214] The historical-critical and reception-historical goals of

---

[207] On attempts to make Christians appear acceptable to Hellene, see DeVore, "Character and Convention."

[208] For Polyhistor's biography, see Sterling, *Historiography and Self-Definition*, 144–152; Carriker, *The Library*.

[209] Suetonius, *Gramm.* 20; Pliny, *Nat.*, 1.3–7, 9, 12–13, 16, 36–37; 9.115; 36.79.

[210] Blakely, "Alexandros Polyhistor." Polyhistor also importantly preserved fragments of Berossos's *Babyloniaca*.

[211] Eusebius, *Praep. ev.* 9.17.1–40.1; Clement, *Strom.* 1.21.130.3.

[212] See Collins, *Between Athens and Jerusalem*, 46–50.

[213] Holladay, *Hellenistic Jewish Literature*; Gruen, *Fragmentary Jewish Historians*.

[214] Ahearne-Kroll, "Constructing Jewish Identity"; Bartlett, *Jews in the Hellenistic World*.

much modern scholarship on ancient Mediterranean religions works to reconstruct the Hellenistic Jewish authors as independent authorial figures who represent a snapshot of the reception of biblical narrative in the Greek East.

Eusebius, however, does not provide much detail about the figures that we typically call the Hellenistic Jewish authors in the *Preparation*.[215] Scholars have even questioned whether we can determine if some of these writers are Jewish or simply wrote about Jewish texts and history, because Eusebius's *Preparation* provides so little context about them. This lack of context is not helped by the fact that the *Preparation* "furnishes perhaps the least secure evidence of firsthand usage of sources," mostly citing writings mediated secondhand through other authors.[216] Eusebius's citational strategies and deployment of author function make it difficult to speak to what we might consider his "primary" sources – but we might turn our attention elsewhere to learn about the citational intermediaries Eusebius relies upon.

Eusebius does not speak about most of these writers independently of Polyhistor's citations, but subsumes them into his portrayal and citational usage of Polyhistor. Unlike scholars' interest in reconstructing the lives, texts, and scriptural hermeneutics of some of our earliest orthonymous Jewish authors, Eusebius treats their names as ammunition that proves the learnedness of Polyhistor. In short: Eusebius and modern scholars have divergent interests in the function of orthonyms in the *Preparation*. While some seek the names of "real" Jewish authors in the sea of pseudonymous and anonymous Jewish literature, Eusebius has a different purpose for preserving particular authorial attributions in his writing. Consequently, Eusebius limits how we might recover historical details because Jewish authors function for him to demonstrate that Hellenes knew about (and spoke positively about) Jews and Jewish literature.

Before turning to Eusebius's use of Polyhistor and the naming of Hellenistic Jewish authors, it is worth pausing on the citational techniques of other historians, ethnographers, and compilers to better contextualize how citations function for Eusebius's own historical and apologetic argument. While much scholarship has been focused on determining how reliable ancient citations are and how to distinguish between citation, paraphrase, and allusion,[217] here I am focused on the function of citationality. So much work has already been done on the *Preparation*, much like Athenaeus's *Deipnosophists,* that treats the text like a "quarry, from which fragments of earlier texts can be hacked out and put to use, perhaps re-arranged."[218] Such an approach treats compilated texts as

---

²¹⁵ On Eusebius's knowledge of Jewish writers, see Carriker, *The Library*, 155–178.
²¹⁶ Carriker, *The Library*, 51–53, quote on 51.
²¹⁷ Fehling, *Herodotus and His "Sources"*; Olson, "Athenaeus' 'Fragments'."
²¹⁸ Braund and Wilkins, "Introductory Remarks," 1.

mirrors into an earlier period whose value is primarily determined by their proximity to modern standards of textual accuracy. What is gained instead by focusing on the act of citing sources, and particularly the act of *naming* one's sources?

Early in Greek historiography, naming of one's sources was common and possible, but not always the most used or useful historiographical approach in order to confirm one's account. Herodotus often relied on oral historical accounts or eyewitnesses, as did other classical Greek historians who distrusted documents and preferred oral witnesses. In this earlier period, we find less of the citing of *texts* in Greek historiography and ethnography, and more the citing of *people.* Vivienne Gray's analysis of Greek historians' use of citations, for example, shows that Herodotus generally named his sources but Thucydides and Xenophon tended to be more opaque.[219] She argues that Thucydides deployed an anonymous "it is said" (λέγεται) in particular situations to qualify and confirm the events as another voice alongside his own, and that citations functioned primarily to "validate content that the reader might find too great to be believed."[220] Gray's work elucidates how early Greek citational strategies were not straightforward attempts to directly and accurately name a source, but that citations functioned rhetorically at the writer's behest.

In the Hellenistic era, we encounter an epistemological and literary shift in which writers produce chronicles, encyclopedias, and compilations based increasingly on textual sources. Historians in particular become more bibliophilic, often citing previously written texts and situating their own work within a broader textual universe. For example, Diodorus Siculus's first-century BCE *Library of History* opens with Diodorus situating himself among those who attempted to produce "universal histories" and yet promulgated errors.[221] Diodorus goes on to ethnically code history as something that contributes to "the power of reason [...] for by this the Hellenes are superior to the barbarians and the educated to the uneducated."[222] Reason is a prominent theme in Eusebius's *Preparation* as well, as Eusebius defends Christianity against accusations that it is irrational or inferior to Hellenic philosophy and culture.

While Diodorus did not begin by listing his sources by name, he lamented the bookish problem of compiling such an encyclopedic account:

> The reason for this is that, first, it is not easy for those who propose to go
> through the writings of so many historians (τὰς τῶν τοσούτων συγγραφέων

---

[219] Gray, "Thucydides' Source Citations," 75.

[220] Gray, "Thucydides' Source Citations," 76; Gray, "Interventions and Citations," 116–117, respectively.

[221] Diodorus Siculus, *Lib.* 1.1.1–4, 1.4.1–2, quote on 1.1.1.

[222] Diodorus Siculus, *Lib.* 1.2.5–6.

ἱστορίας) to produce the books (βίβλων) which come to be needed, and second, because of their irregularity and numerousness (διὰ τὴν ἀνωμαλίαν καὶ τὸ πλῆθος), the recovery of past events becomes extremely difficult for comprehension and attainment.[223]

Diodorus not only depicted his own *Library* as the culmination of previous historical accounts, but also underscored that his project required amassing innumerable amounts of textual data that needed to be streamlined for his readership.[224] Eusebius does not explicitly frame the *Preparation* around the consumption and consolidation of bookish knowledge like Diodorus, but rather treats such encyclopedic accounts as authoritative. Eusebius's first substantial quotation in the *Preparation* is Diodorus's *Library,* written by "a man well known to the most educated of the Hellenes."[225] Rather than telling, Eusebius shows his readers the substantial research undertaken to write the *Preparation.*

Roman Mediterranean writers often frontloaded their historical works with a list of sources to reveal how they classified authors and knowledge. For example, Pliny's first book of the *Natural History,* often overlooked for its pedantry, is dedicated wholly to classifying the following books' sources: Latin authorities (*ex auctoribus*) and other authorities (*ex externis*). Pliny's work is encyclopedic and taxonomized in a way that "frames knowledge for consumption by a Roman audience."[226] Latin writers like Marcus Varro, Cornelius Nepos, and the emperor Titus are characterized merely as "authors" (*auctores*) from which Pliny pulls (*ex auctoribus*), whereas writers like Herodotus, Posidonius, and Polyhistor are depicted as foreigners ([*ex*] *externis* [*auctoribus*]).[227] Even Alexander Polyhistor, who lived much of his life in Rome and became a prominent local historian, is categorized as a foreigner by Pliny since he was trafficked from Asia Minor and wrote primarily in Greek. Similarly, Varro's *On Agriculture* divides authors and knowledge based on language and birthplace. He opens the treatise with "those who wrote in Greek [. . .] whom you can call to your aid" in one category, along with "the rest, whose home countries I have not learned."[228] Knowledge and the writer's citation of authors is ethnically coded, such that Greek knowledge, Latin knowledge, and Jewish knowledge become salient in for writers' particular circumstances and agendas.[229]

---

[223] Diodorus Siculus, *Lib.* 1.3.8.   [224] Cf. Luke 1:1–4.

[225] Eusebius, *Praep. ev* 1.6.9; cf. Diodorus Siculus, *Lib.* 1.6–8.

[226] Murphy, *Pliny the Elder,* 29.   [227] Pliny the Elder, *Nat.* 1.2.

[228] Varro, *Rust.* 1.8–9. Varro goes on to classify his remarks based on what he has practiced on his own land, what he read, and what he has heard from experts (1.11). Cf. Columella, *Rust.* 1.7–14.

[229] Jansari, "From Geography to Paradoxography," who demonstrates various different generic and apologetic rationales (e.g., ethnography, Jewish & Indian philosophical details, paradoxography) that the *Indica* survives even in citational, fragmentary form.

Eusebius's *Preparation*, like Pliny and Varro, categorized knowledge production along ethnic lines, especially regarding the different knowledge bases Hellenes and Jews pull from: Hellenic philosophy and Jewish scripture.[230] Eusebius arranged the *Preparation* both to distinguish these knowledge bases when convenient, and to blend them when he wanted to demonstrate Hellenic appreciation of Jewish history. For example, *Praep. ev.* 6 is dedicated to Hellenic interest oracles and fate, which Eusebius refutes as demonically influenced, while *Praep. ev.* 7–8 focuses on the lives of the ancient Jews and cites Philo, Josephus, Aristobulus, and Aristeas. *Praep. ev.* 9, however, turns to "the most illustrious of the Hellenes themselves" (αὐτῶν Ἑλλήνων οἱ μάλιστα διαφανεῖς) as a distinct ethnic group whose conception of Jews is worth investigating in its own right.[231] In order to prove the rationality of Christianity to a previously Hellenic audience, Eusebius demonstrates that Hellenic philosophers and historians themselves found Jewish history, texts, and authors worth talking about.

Finally, it is worth pointing that the *Preparation* has notable similarities in its citational strategy to Athenaeus's *Deipnosophists*. The *Deipnosophists* is a complex early third-century text that depicts a series of sympotic discussions, considered invaluable for its extensive citation of otherwise-lost authors and texts. Athenaeus opens the text by depicting himself as the "father of the book" who "in these does not omit anyone's best sayings."[232] Athenaeus fits well into the Roman imperial concern with written records, as he functions "as a reader and as a scholar deeply concerned with the collecting, identifying and classifying of books, as well as with reading and browsing through them."[233] We find that Athenaeus – much like Eusebius – often lacks anonymous citations, but rather is keen on providing authors' names, titles, and book numbers. Both writers find it important to demonstrate their breadth of textual knowledge, to become a type of "walking library."[234] Athenaeus and Eusebius are coincidentally two of the only writers that heavily use Diodorus's *Library* in the late Roman period, and are likely mimicking his encyclopedic approach to universal bookish knowledge.[235] Both writers decide what knowledge is worth preserving and whose names ought to be remembered through their citational approach.

Now to turn to Polyhistor and his use of Jewish writers as re-presented by Eusebius. Polyhistor's preservation of Hellenistic Jewish authors' names is often heralded as an important moment for the reconstruction of Hellenistic

---

[230] See Eusebius, *Praep. ev.* 1.2 for a list of questions and arguments that Eusebius expects both Hellenes and Jews will have about Christian innovation, illogicity, or misunderstanding of Jewish scripture.

[231] Eusebius, *Praep. ev.* 9.1.1. Greek text from Schroeder and Places, *Eusèbe de Césarée*.

[232] Athenaeus, *Deipn.* 1.1a.   [233] Jacob, "Athenaeus the Librarian," 86.

[234] Too, "The Walking Library," 113.

[235] Inowlocki, *Eusebius*, 207–209; Jacob, "Athenaeus the Librarian," 102.

Jewish culture and the history of authorship in Jewish literature. The names of these authors are often taken at face value and used to celebrate, for example, "the discovery of the individuality of the author" in the Hellenistic era and the conjoining of a long history of Jewish anonymity with Hellenistic orthonymity.[236] The same association between Hellenistic models of authorship and Jewish texts appears in scholarship on the second-century BCE *Ben Sira* as one of our first orthonymous Jewish authors.[237] As noted in conversation with Wright and Mroczek's characterization of *Ben Sira* as pseudo-pseudepigraphy in Section 1, we might question whether the influence of Hellenic authorial norms is primarily responsible for the so-called birth of the Jewish author. Additionally, we might interrogate Hengel's presumption that orthonymity is required for authors to gain a sense of "individuality," since such a characterization may misleadingly suggest that pseudonymous and anonymous writers were so enmeshed in collectivist cultures that they could not imagine themselves as independent selves (according to Western standards of autonomy and individualism).

Rather than reconstructing why orthonymity would have emerged among third-/second-century BCE Jewish authors, however, I want to ask how these names are put to use where they are actually preserved by early Christians: why does Eusebius name his citations of Hellenistic Jewish authors via Polyhistor, and how do they function to further the purpose of the *Preparation*? Hellenistic Jewish authors like Ezekiel, Eupolemus, and Artapanus are not merely taking on orthonymous authorial roles under the umbrella of Hellenistic literary culture, but are received as citable because of their association with Polyhistor. Eusebius's approach to citing these Jewish authors fits well with a question asked by Richard Goulet: whether Diogenes Laertius's citations in the *Lives and Opinions of Eminent Philosophers* are meant to function as sources for his biographies, or simply that his citations' authority can be put to use.[238] Similarly, Eusebius's citations are framed not based on how their interpretations of Jewish history or literature might impact Eusebius's audience, but as evidence pointed toward a polymath Polyhistor.

Many of the so-called "minor Jewish writers" – poets, historians, and other writers of the Hellenistic era – survive thirdhand. Polyhistor preserves fragmentary accounts of these Jewish writers' works because of what William Adler calls Polyhistor's "slavish attachment to written documents."[239] Like Josephus's lament that Greek historiography and record-keeping is all so modern in comparison to the Chaldaeans, Egyptians, Phoenicians, and

---

[236] Hengel, *Die Evangelienüberschriften*, 25.
[237] Mack, *Wisdom and the Hebrew Epic*, 186–187.   [238] Goulet, "Les références."
[239] Adler, "Alexander Polyhistor's *Peri Ioudaiōn*," 230–233, quote on 230.

Judeans,[240] the bookish Polyhistor seemed to have been attracted to writing about Judeans because of their extensive written culture, which was becoming increasingly accessible to Greek speakers by the second century BCE. Polyhistor's writing emerges in the midst of Roman colonial expansion and ethnographic writing that sought to explain, classify, (sometimes) assimilate, and control the "other" through understanding their practices and heritage.[241]

These citations are one form of *extradiegetic* orthonymity, since the names of these Hellenistic Jewish authors are only used and preserved by later writers rather than being explicitly integral to (and internal to) the authors' own texts in their extant form. This is, in part, why the Hellenistic Jewish historians and other writers used by Eusebius and Polyhistor stick out, because they purportedly preserve the names of these early Jewish writers. However, I want to caution against too quickly asserting how these authors used their names in their own third- and second-century BCE contexts, since we do not have access to that layer of their dissemination or reception. Instead, we only have how Polyhistor (and, later, Josephus, Clement, and Eusebius) used their names in their own historical and apologetic works, and so can most robustly speak about author function only centuries after their composition.

While we do not know exactly why Polyhistor wrote *On the Jews* and preserved the names of various Jewish writers, we have more tangible evidence for Eusebius's decision to preserve their names in the *Preparation*. These historians, poets, and other writers only survive thirdhand because they are tangentially useful to Eusebius's broader project: to demonstrate via Polyhistor, a respected Hellenic historian, that Hellenic writers themselves admire Jewish history and literature. As Sabrina Inowlocki argues, Eusebius's *Preparation* focuses on the authors cited and the dispositions of such authors rather than on the content: "[Eusebius] deems the book important only because it conveys the voice of its author."[242] I agree and argue that Eusebius is only marginally interested in the names of some of our earliest orthonymous Jewish writers, since his main goal is to demonstrate Polyhistor's reliability and utilize that reliability for his apologetic project. For Eusebius, the voice of Jewish authors matters inasmuch as they bolster Polyhistor's profile among his Hellenic readers and recent converts.

Since the *Preparation* is primarily meant as a pedagogical tool and library-encapsulated-in-a-book for newly converted Hellenes (*Praep. ev.* 1.1), how does citing Hellenistic Jewish authors – or more broadly, any authors – by name help bolster Eusebius's argument that Christians are rational readers and

---

[240] Josephus, *C. Ap.* 1.6–14.
[241] Too, *The Idea of the Library*. Cf. Berzon, *Classifying Christians*, 61–66.
[242] Inowlocki, *Eusebius*, 205.

practitioners? Eusebius notes outright that Jewish scriptures will not benefit the solidification of faith of Hellenes:

> From what source then shall we verify our proofs? Not, of course, from our own scriptures, lest we should seem to show favor to our argument. But let Hellenes themselves appear as our witnesses, both those of them who boast of their philosophy, and those who have investigated the history of other nations.[243]

Instead of relying on what he deems the library of insiders, Eusebius turns to the library of outsiders to demonstrate the truth of his Christian message and its continuity with ancient Hebrew (*not* contemporaneous Jewish) doctrines.[244] This strategy to convince formerly pagan readers climaxes in *Praep. ev.* 9, where Eusebius surveys a wide range of Greek authors (Polyhistor, Berossus, Abydenus, Numenius, Choerilus, Clearchus, Theophrastus). After his examination of the reliability of Hebrew oracles over Hellenic ones, he sets out the goals of *Praep. ev.* 9 to demonstrate "that even the most illustrious of the Hellenes themselves have not been unacquainted with the deeds of the Hebrews, but some of them testified to the truth of the historical narratives among them as well as the life of their men."[245] Perhaps most importantly, Eusebius desires to show "how many of the Hellenic historians have mentioned *by name* both Jews and Hebrews" (δεικνὺς ὅσοι τῶν ἑλληνικῶν συγγραφέων ἐπ᾿ ὀνόματος Ἰουδαίων τε καὶ Ἑβραίων).[246] Notably, Eusebius expresses interest here not in proving that Hellenic historians knew the names of and were citing Hellenistic Jewish authors *per se*, but rather in proving that these Hellenic historians knew the names of biblical figures (e.g., Moses, Abraham). In other words, orthonymity of Jewish writers was deemed less important than demonstrating Hellenic knowledge of Jewish texts. For example, Eusebius notes how Polyhistor "arranges the deeds of this man Abraham in the following manner," emphasizing Polyhistor's knowledge of *Abraham* rather than the fact that his knowledge is mediated through Eupolemus's *On the Jews of Assyria*.[247] Onymity matters, but Hellenistic Jewish orthonymity is almost an afterthought for the *Preparation* compared to the names of biblical figures.

Eusebius seeks to demonstrate to his Hellenic audience that his sources are independent of his own Christian bias. Diodorus, one of his most substantial sources in *Praep. ev.* 1, is recounted as being a great figure who collected native Egyptian historical works (e.g., Manetho's *Aegyptiaca*) in order to prove that

---

²⁴³ Eusebius, *Praep. ev.* 1.6.8.; Cf. 1.5.14; Inowlocki, *Eusebius*, 55–56.

²⁴⁴ On Eusebius's distinction between Hebrews and Jews, see Inowlocki, *Eusebius*, 105–138; Johnson, *Ethnicity and Argument*; Jacobs, "A Jew's Jew," esp. 276–280.

²⁴⁵ Eusebius, *Praep. ev.* 9.1.1.　　²⁴⁶ Eusebius, *Praep. ev.* 9.1.2, emphasis mine.

²⁴⁷ Eusebius, *Praep. ev.* 9.17.1.

Hellenic theology was derivative of earlier, non-Hellenic material.[248] Hecataeus of Abdera, a fourth-century BCE Hellenic historian, is likewise described by Eusebius as a prominent philosophy and "competent in active life," who wrote about Jews and is preserved via Josephus.[249] Perhaps one of the clearest moments of Eusebius avoiding his own authorial voice occurs in his critique of oracles in *Praep. ev.* 5, in which he cites Oenomaus's *The Detection of Imposters,* with which he provides an exhortation: "from whose own voices, and not mine, listen."[250] Eusebius even goes so far as to cite authors that he wholeheartedly disagrees with – such as Porphyry of Tyre, a student of the famous Neoplatonist Plotinus, and Sanchuniathon's *Phoenician History* – to prove that even Porphyry is occasionally capable of reading the correct type of texts.[251] As Inowlocki demonstrates, Eusebius's Hellenic testimonies underscore his own historical accuracy and rhetorical legitimacy: "The selected authors are presented in a favourable light because, on the one hand, they guarantee the apologist's demonstration, and on the other, their authority in pagan milieus had to be emphasized in order to be taken into account by pagan readers."[252] By stressing how his curation of quotations are reliable and speak for themselves, Eusebius attempts to disguise his own *compilative* voice and his own depiction of Hellenic writers as trustworthy recorders. Polyhistor himself is given high praise in order to secure his spot as a reliable source:

> Alexander Polyhistor, a man of great intellect and much learning, and very well known to those Hellenes who have gathered the fruits of education in no perfunctory manner; for in his compilation *On the Jews,* he records the history of this man Abraham in the following manner word for word.[253]

Polyhistor is underscored as reliable, in part, because of his recognizability among Hellenes and his Hellenic education – not to mention Eusebius's own compilative self-deprecation, emphasized through how he claims to record Polyhistor verbatim rather than inserting his own words.

Elsewhere in the *Preparation*, Eusebius is careful to note whether his cited authors are Hebrew, Hellenic, or something else. While often grouped together with the "minor Jewish authors," Aristobulus of Alexandria is known to Eusebius independently of Polyhistor's *On the Jews* and is cited especially alongside Philo in *Praep. ev.* 7 as an authority regarding God's co-worker in creation). Eusebius portrays Aristobulus as "another wise man of the Hebrews

---

[248] Eusebius, *Praep. ev.* 1.7, 2.1–2.   [249] Eusebius, *Praep. ev.* 9.4.

[250] Eusebius, *Praep. ev.* 5.18.6.

[251] Eusebius, *Praep. ev.* 1.9. Eusebius highlights how Sanchuiathon's work is more reliable and older than all Hellenic poets and historians, and so goes beyond the work of fable or poetry (1.10; 2.pref).

[252] Inowlocki, *Eusebius*, 75.   [253] Eusebius, *Praep. ev.* 9.17.

(ἄλλος Ἑβραίων σοφὸς ἀνήρ), who flourished under the rule of the Ptolemies, [who] confirms the doctrine as inherited from his fathers," since he records what Aristobulus calls the "opinions of the Hebrews" (παρ' Ἑβραίοις).[254] He is treated as an authorial figure who bridges the gap between Aristotelian and Hebrew philosophical systems.[255] Likewise, Eusebius depicts Philo as a representative of Hebrew thought: "a Hebrew man (Ἑβραῖον ἄνδρα), who received from his forefathers an accurate knowledge of his own history, and had learned the doctrine from his teachers."[256] Like Aristobulus, Philo's ethnicity and upbringing confirms his reliability on the topic. Josephus is also treated as "Josephus the Hebrew" (Ἰωσήπου τοῦ Ἑβραίου) by Eusebius, as a representative of Hebrew writers that prove the relative youth of Hellenic thought.[257] Even John the evangelist is painted by Eusebius as a "Hebrew from the Hebrews" (Ἑβραῖος ὤν ἐξ Ἑβραίων).[258] Amelius, a student of Plotinus and obsessive reader of Numenius's treatises, cites John 1 as the work of an anonymous barbarian philosopher, which gives Eusebius leeway to re-characterize John the evangelist alongside other figures as Hebrew – here, meaning one of the "pure, monotheistic people of God who shared in the faith of Abraham before the time of Moses."[259] Eusebius is calculating not only in his curation of citations and authors, but also in his characterization of particular authors as Hebrews, bound to and representative of a pre-Mosaic lineage of proper piety.

Polyhistor's Hellenistic Jewish writers, however, do not all receive the same commendation from Eusebius, as Table 1 maps out. Those who are not labeled as either Hebrews or Jews, coincidentally, are most of the "minor Jewish authors" whose names are preserved by Eusebius via Polyhistor. *Praep. ev.* 9 opens with Eusebius underscoring how he will show the range of Greek historians that mention Jews and Hebrews by name, but his use of Polyhistor's work suggests that the Jewish and Hebrew figures whose names he is trying to access are ancient: Abraham, Jacob, and Moses. Eusebius's interest falls at times not on the historians, philosophers, and poets, but on the fact that a notable Hellenic historian had paid attention to "Hebrew" narratives as mediated by earlier historians. Unlike with Aristobulus, Josephus, Philo of Alexandria, or John the evangelist, Eusebius never independently provides the

---

254 Eusebius, *Praep. ev.* 7.13.7 and 7.14.2; cf. 13.11. Greek text from Schroeder, *Eusèbe de Césarée.*

255 Eusebius, *Praep. ev.* 8.9.   256 Eusebius, *Praep. ev.* 7.12.14; cf. 7.20; 11.14–15.

257 Eusebius, *Praep. ev.* 10.6.15, 10.12. Cf. Jacobs, "A Jew's Jew," 279 on how Josephus is treated as both a "Jew" and a "Hebrew" in such a way that Eusebius might imagine him to be a crypto-Christian.

258 Eusebius, *Praep. ev.* 11.19.2. Greek text from Favrelle, *Eusèbe de Césarée.*

259 Jacobs, "A Jew's Jew," 276. Such characterizations of a pre-Jewish monotheism in Israelite culture that some Jews and Christians (and pagans) can be classified within is a shared rhetorical strategy with Epiphanius. See Chalmers, "Past Paul's Jewishness."

Table 1 Citations and Characterizations of Hellenistic Jewish Writers.

Author	Citation	Characterization by Eusebius
Aristobulus	Eusebius, *Praep. ev.* 8.9.38, 13.11.3 Eusebius, *Hist. eccl.* 7.32 Clement, *Strom.* 1.15, 5.14	Partaker of Aristotle's philosophy and of Judean philosophy Hebrew philosopher
Eupolemus	Eusebius, *Praep. ev.* 9.17–18, 9.26.1, 9.30–34, 9.42.3 Eusebius, *Hist. eccl.* 6.13.7 Jerome, *Vir ill.* 38 Clement, *Strom.* 1.23.153, 1.21.130 Josephus, *C. Ap.* 1.23	Writer of *On the Jews of Assyria*
Artapanus	Eusebius, *Praep. ev.* 9.18.1, 9.23.1, 9.27.1 Clement, *Strom.* 1.23.154	Writer of *On the Jews*
Philo the Elder	Eusebius, *Praep. ev.* 9.20.1, 9.24.1, 9.37.1 Clement, *Strom.* 1.21.141 Josephus, *C. Ap.* 1.23	Writer of *On Jerusalem*
Cleodemus/ Malchus	Eusebius, *Praep. ev.* 9.20.3 Josephus, *Ant.* 1.15	Prophet
Demetrius the Chronographer	Eusebius, *Praep. ev.* 9.21.1, 9.29.1–3, 9.29.15 Clement, *Strom.* 1.21.141 Josephus, *C. Ap.* 1.23	Writer
Theodotus	Eusebius, *Praep. ev.* 9.22.1	Writer of *On the Jews*
Aristeas the Exegete	Eusebius, *Praep. ev.* 9.25.1, 9.38.1	Writer of *On the Jews* Writer of *On the Interpretation of the Laws of the Jews*
Ezekiel the Tragedian	Eusebius, *Praep. ev.* 9.28.1, 9.29.4–16 Clement, *Strom.* 1.23.155–56	Tragic poet Writer of drama *The Exodus*
[Thallus]	Josephus, *Ant.* 18.6.4 Theophilus, *Autol.* 3.29	N/A in Eusebius

names or comments on the texts of the Hellenistic Jewish authors used by Polyhistor. In fact, Howard Jacobson suggests that in some instances Eusebius may not know the works of Hellenistic Jewish authors independently from

Polyhistor.[260] These orthonyms are almost incidental to Eusebius's goal of excavating Polyhistor's *On the Jews* and its use of earlier historians to prove Hellenic interest in and respect for Jewish history and narrative.

The lack of "Jewishness" attributed to Polyhistor's minor Jewish authors has led to a divide in scholarly interpretation of the data. If Polyhistor was Eusebius's only vantage point by which he knew of authors like Demetrius and Ezekiel, did he know or believe that they were Jewish writers in the first place? Some, like Gregory Sterling, argue that Eusebius knew these writers were Jewish and simply failed to mention it in the *Preparation*.[261] This perspective is bolstered by how Eusebius labels many of these writers as Jewish in his recounting of Clement of Alexandria's works in the *Ecclesiastical History*:

> Moreover, [Clement mentions] Philo and Aristobulus and Josephus and Demetrius and Eupolemus, Jewish writers (Ἰουδαίων συγγραφέων), since they would all show in writing that Moses and the Jewish race went back further in their origins than the Hellenes.[262]

On the other hand, Louis Feldman argues that Eusebius did not consider these writers Jewish, but instead believed that Josephus was the first Jewish historian.[263] This has led to some debate among those who study Hellenistic Jewish historians to ask whether we ought to presume that anyone writing about Jewish narratives and histories must be Jewish, or if it is possible for others to write such accounts as well.[264] Inowlocki takes a middle ground between these two perspectives, arguing that Eusebius seems to find the identity of these minor writers irrelevant:

> Strikingly, Eusebius never clarifies the religious identity of the minor Jewish authors who are extensively used in book IX of the *Praeparatio,* nor does he seem to pay any attention to it either. He is, rather, more interested in the fact that it is through them that Alexander Polyhistor knew biblical history. On this occasion, he presents him as an erudite man whose works had a determining influence on Greek culture.[265]

I agree with Inowlocki that Eusebius simply is not interested in the authorship of these Jewish histories, provided that they are fodder for a more respectable (by Hellenic standards) historian. If Eusebius did know that Polyhistor's sources were Jewish authors, their Jewishness was in fact

---

[260] Jacobson, "Eusebius."   [261] Sterling, *Historiography,* 282–284.
[262] Eusebius, *Hist. eccl.* 6.13.7.   [263] Feldman, *Jew and Gentile,* 207.
[264] For example, Jacobson, "Artapanus Judaeus," argues that Artapanus was a non-Jewish Hellenic historian. Similarly, Walsh (*Origins,* 105–133) suggests that the New Testament gospel writers need not be (exclusively) Christ-followers.
[265] Inowlocki, *Eusebius,* 274–277, quote on 274.

a potential deterrent, since his goal in the *Preparation* was to prepare and convince newly converted Hellenes to accept Christian hermeneutics of Hebrew scriptures based on *Hellenic* testimonies. As noted earlier, the *Preparation* was written by Eusebius as a guide "for our new converts from the nations" (τοῖς ἐξ ἐθνῶν ἄρτι προσιοῦσιν) as an elementary introduction (στοιχειώσεως καὶ εἰσαγωγῆς) before they encountered arguments from Jewish texts.[266] Perhaps Eusebius purposefully did not clarify their identities, since his point was that Polyhistor is a good Hellene who wrote feverishly about Jews and recorded earlier writers who similarly took deep interest in Jewish history and interpretation. In Eusebius's quoting of Polyhistor, it's noticeable that Polyhistor does not do much to differentiate between what we might consider pro-Jewish authors (i.e., Artapanus) and anti-Jewish authors (i.e., Apollonius Molon), since his goal is to record what earlier ethnographic and historical writers have said about Jewish origins and stories. Eusebius followed Polyhistor's lead, since his own rhetorical goals for the *Preparation* depended on the *orthonymity* but not the religio-ethnic identity of Polyhistor's sources.

Eusebius's arrangement of the *Preparation* and *Demonstration* itself depends on what he deems the Hellenic Christian's supersessionist evolutionary development from Hellenism to Judaism to Christianity. Eusebius notes in *Praep. ev.* 1 that he and his audience are "Hellenes by race, and Hellenes in their thought" (τὸ γένος Ἕλληνες ὄντες καὶ τὰ Ἑλλήνων φρονοῦντες) who "abandoned the ancestral superstition" by adhering to "Jewish books" (ταῖς ἰουδαικαῖς βίβλοις) and developing doctrines out of them.[267] However, he notes that some Jewish customs (e.g., circumcision) are also seen as developmentally prior to "proper" Christianity and ought to be abandoned. To parallel this trajectory, the two-part book is written so as to prove that Hellenic authors and Jewish scripture should be used as *part of* but not the final goal of Christian literature, thought, and practice. What Eusebius considers Jewish books are scriptural texts shared with Jewish practitioners, and Hellenic texts as those written by prominent Greek historians; the "minor Jewish historians," however, end up in a gray zone in Eusebius's Hellenism → Judaism → Christianity mapping of proper socioreligious development.

Writers like Porphyry, whom Eusebius called "that very friend of the demons,"[268] are a helpful example of Eusebius's call for readers to fact-check his sources. At various points, Eusebius calls on readers to examine a text alongside him, consider the line of argumentation for themselves, or read

---

[266] Eusebius, *Praep. ev.* 1.1.12.   [267] Eusebius, *Praep. ev.* 1.5.10.
[268] Eusebius, *Praep. ev.* 4.6.1.

the same sources he is (e.g., Porphyry's *Epistle of Anebo the Egyptian*).[269] However, it's unclear whether Eusebius actually expected his recent Hellenic converts to seek out the texts he cites to confirm his reading. When discussing Jesus's letter to Abgar of Edessa in the *Ecclesiastical History*, Eusebius claims that there is a "documentary witness" of this narrative in the Edessan archives that have "been found preserved down to the present."[270] As Gregory Given notes, Eusebius uses this rhetorical maneuver to claim that anyone could fact-check him when "in fact, the expectation is that most readers would not have the means to do so."[271] A similar citational game plays out in the *Preparation*, in which Eusebius calls on his readers to fact-check him and his use of Hellenic sources as a persuasive attempt to convince new converts that Eusebius's citations *and interpretations of these citations* are valid.

Eusebius's citational use of Polyhistor and the "minor Jewish historians" by extension might be understood, as Inowlocki suggests, as a method to "establish a cultural complicity with the reader" and for the "preservation of cultural continuity."[272] Eusebius's stance differs especially from that of Josephus, who critiqued the first-century consensus that Hellenic historians ought to be deemed trustworthy and instead suggested that their more ancient counterparts (e.g., Egyptians, Chaldaeans, Phoenicians, Jews) have a more robust historical record and are more reliable sources.[273] By contrast, Eusebius claims Hellenic ethnic and cultural heritage as his own (and presumes the same for his newly converted readers), and so does not denigrate the relative youth of Hellenic or Roman historiographical traditions as does Josephus. Rather, he paints a picture of Polyhistor as a knowledgeable Hellene whose trustworthiness stems in part from his willingness and ability to compile earlier historiographical and literary sources about Jews. Polyhistor becomes, in a way, a reflection of how Eusebius imagines his own compilative approach in the *Preparation*, since Polyhistor's own learnedness can rub off on Eusebius through his extensive citations.

The Hellenistic Jewish authors that Eusebius name-drops via Polyhistor have often been understood, much like *Ben Sira*, to be the product of a Hellenistic shift in naming oneself as a writer and a growing practice of classifying texts under orthonyms. I think that this is partially correct, but not the entire story. In the midst of historians ethnically coding and classifying the texts and authors from whom they cite, Eusebius spotlights Polyhistor's Greekness while not

---

[269] Eusebius, *Praep. ev.* 4.6.1, 5.1, 5.7. Occasionally, Eusebius sneaks in Christian writers (e.g., Bardaisan; Origen in *Praep. ev.* 6.9–11) other than himself that he claims are unbiased interpreters of difficult passages.

[270] Given, "Utility and Variance," 194; Eusebius, *Hist. eccl.* 1.13.5.

[271] Given, "Utility and Variance," 194n22; Jacob, "Athenaeus the Librarian," 90–91.

[272] Inowlocki, *Eusebius*, 38.   [273] Josephus, *C. Ap.* 1.pref.2.

emphasizing the Jewishness of those Polyhistor cites. Eusebius depends on his name-dropping of Polyhistor – and, by extension, Polyhistor's name-dropping of earlier historians – to demonstrate that both he and his sources are trustworthy and persuasive in proving that Hellenes themselves already recognize the importance of Jewish history and literature.

In his attempt to make the *Preparation* a miniature library – "a book encompassing other books, read, summarized, and paraphrased"[274] – Eusebius's focus is not necessarily on the Jewish writers. Perhaps frustratingly for contemporary scholars, Eusebius's thirdhand preservation of the names of those we consider some of our earliest orthonymous Jewish writers in the Hellenistic period is almost incidental, or at least not something that Eusebius intended to do for the same reasons that excite scholars of Hellenistic Judaism. In the case of the *Preparation*, the minor Jewish historians are names and texts put to use for Eusebius's apologetic goals in a way that preserves orthonyms that otherwise may have been lost along with Polyhistor's *On the Jews*. Here, attribution of "correct" authorship matters only inasmuch as it demonstrates Hellenic and Christian bookishness and attentiveness to Jewish history and literature.

Conclusion

My aim in this Element has been twofold: to proliferate the authors that we see by smudging the supposedly transparent window of orthonymity, and to suggest that even using "correct" authorial names is not a default but rather a choice made for specific purposes.

I want to end with two final thoughts on the figure of the author and its effects. The first is that my scare-quotes throughout this Element around terms like "correct," "proper," "real," and "right" highlight the contingency of authorial attribution. To remove these scare-quotes requires fully unpacking *for whom* and *for what purposes* a writer applies a particular name to a particular text. In doing so, we might continually ask more specific questions about the deployment of authorial attribution based on a writer's or tradent's goals (inasmuch as we can know them). Transmitting an epistle as Paul's is "correct" in a different way for Paul himself than it is, for example, for the writer of the *Acts of Paul and Thecla* whom Tertullian claimed wrote "out of love for Paul" (*amore Pauli*), or for the writer of the *Epistle to the Laodicaeans* who created a patchwork of other Pauline+ epistles.[275] Correctness of authorial attribution is situationally contingent and ought to be treated as such when we examine ancient Mediterranean literature – especially since we often know so little

---

[274] Jacob, "Athenaeus the Librarian," 102.

[275] Tertullian, *Bapt.* 17; Nasrallah, "Out of Love for Paul"; Walsh, "The *Epistle to the Laodiceans*."

about the motivations of ancient writers. Consequently, orthonymity ends up not being the default or universally right way to attribute any given text, but instead reveals historically and ideologically bound classificatory parameters. There is much at stake in the twenty-first century regarding whether or not New Testament epistles contain Paul's very words, or regarding the limits of "cherry-picking" biblical passages.

My second point is that where there is classification, there are often hierarchies of knowledge.[276] The author, as I mentioned in the introduction, is a container that helps its users delineate acceptable texts, ideas, people, and sources of knowledge. Accordingly, the concept of an author can be put to work to delimit what books can (or cannot) be read, what knowledge readers ought to have access to, and what people one is encouraged to associate with. As Emily Knox argues in her analysis of twenty-first-century book banning in the United States, such censorship emerges out of a desire to control access to particular authorial figures and the types of knowledge they are attached to in "a struggle for domination over who has the authority to determine the boundaries of legitimate and illegitimate knowledge in the public sphere."[277] Book bans in the United States in recent years have especially targeted writers who are queer, non-white, or politically progressive, and assert that their authorial name and contents of their writing are dangerous to the fomentation and preservation of white supremacy and heteropatriarchy.[278] My hope is that more robust analysis of author function in antiquity and modernity will help us challenge how the author can be weaponized to suppress access to knowledge and oppress marginalized people.

---

[276] Lampland and Star, ed., *Standards and Their Stories*; Berzon, *Classifying Christians*.
[277] Knox, *Book Banning*, 28.   [278] Meehan and Friedman, "Banned in the USA."

Bibliography

Achtemeier, Paul J. *1 Peter: A Commentary on First Peter.* Hermeneia. Minneapolis, MN: Fortress Press, 2016.

Adler, William. "Alexander Polyhistor's *Peri Ioudaiōn* and Literary Culture in Republican Rome." Pages 225–240 in *Reconsidering Eusebius: Collected Papers in Literary, Historical, and Theological Issues.* Edited by Sabrina Inowlocki and Claudio Zamagni. VCSupp 107. Leiden: Brill, 2011.

Ahearne-Kroll, Patricia. "Constructing Jewish Identity in Ptolemaic Egypt: The Case of Artapanus." Pages 434–456 in *The "Other" in Second Temple Judaism: Essays in Honor of John J. Collins.* Edited by Daniel C. Harlow, Karina Martin Hogan, Matthew Goff, and Joel S. Kaminsky. Grand Rapids, MI: Eerdmans, 2011.

Aland, Kurt. "The Problem of Anonymity and Pseudonymity in Christian Literature of the First Two Centuries." Pages 1–13 in *The Authorship and Integrity of the New Testament: Some Recent Studies.* Edited by Kurt Aland. London: SPCK, 1965.

Allen, Garrick V. and Anthony P. Royle. "Paratexts Seeking Understanding: Manuscripts and Aesthetic Cognitivism." *Religions* 11 (2020): 1–25.

Askwith, Edward H. "'I' and 'We' in the Thessalonian Epistles." *Expositor* 8.1 (1911): 149–159.

Attridge, Harold W. "Valentinians Reading John." Pages 414–433 in *Valentinianism: New Studies.* Edited by Einar Thomassen and Christoph Markschies. NHMS 96. Leiden: Brill, 2019.

Ayres, Lewis. "Irenaeus vs. the Valentinians: Toward a Rethinking of Patristic Exegetical Origins." *JECS* 23.2 (2015): 153–187.

Bailey, David R. Shackleton. *Anthologia Latina*, vol. 1: *Carmina in codicibus scripta, fasc. 1, Libri Salmasiani aliorumque carmina.* Stuttgart: Teubner, 1982.

Barnes, Timothy D. *Tertullian: A Historical and Literary Study.* Oxford: Clarendon, 1971.

Barrett, Charles K. *The First Epistle to the Corinthians.* HNTC. New York: Harper & Row, 1968.

Barthes, Roland. "The Death of the Author." Pages 277–280 in *The Book History Reader*, 2nd ed. Edited by David Finkelstein and Alistair McCleery. London: Routledge, 2006.

Barthes, Roland. "From Work to Text." Pages 235–241 in *The Novel: An Anthology of Criticism and Theory, 1900–2000*. Edited by Dorothy J. Hale. Malden, MA: Blackwell, 2006.

Bartlett, John R. *Jews in the Hellenistic World: Josephus, Aristeas, Sibylline Oracles, Eupolemus*. Cambridge: Cambridge University Press, 1985.

Baum, Armin D. "The Anonymity of the New Testament History Books: A Stylistic Device in the Context of Greco-Roman and Ancient Near Eastern Literature." *NT* 50 (2008): 120–142.

Behr, John. *Irenaeus of Lyons: Identifying Christianity*. Oxford: Oxford University Press, 2013.

Berzon, Todd. *Classifying Christians: Ethnography, Heresiology, and the Limits of Knowledge in Late Antiquity*. Oakland: University of California Press, 2016.

Bingham, D. Jeffrey. "Paideia and Polemic in Second-Century Lyons: Irenaeus on Education." Pages 323–358 in *Pedagogy in Ancient Judaism and Early Christianity*. Edited by Karina Martin Hogan, Matthew Goff, and Emma Wasserman. Atlanta: SBL Press, 2017.

Birke, Dorothee. "Author, Authority, and 'Authorial Narration': The Eighteenth-Century English Novel as a Test Case." Pages 99–112 in *Author and Narrator: Transdisciplinary Contributions to a Narratological Debate*. Edited by Dorothee Birke and Tilmann Köppe. Berlin: De Gruyter, 2015.

Blakely, Sandra. "Alexandros Polyhistor." *Brill's New Jacoby* 3 (2015): 273 F1–11.

Bloomer, William Martin. *The School of Rome: Latin Studies and the Origins of Liberal Education*. Berkeley: University of California Press, 2011.

Bond, Sarah E. "It's on the Sillybos: The Birth of the Book Title." *History from Below*. May 16, 2016. https://sarahemilybond.com/2016/05/16/its-on-the-sillybos-the-birth-of-the-book-title/.

Brakke, David. "Early Christian Lies and the Lying Liars Who Wrote Them: Bart Ehrman's *Forgery and Counterforgery*." *Journal of Religion* 96.3 (2016): 378–390.

Braund, David and John Wilkins. "Introductory Remarks." Pages 1–2 in *Athenaeus and His World: Reading Greek Culture in the Roman Empire*. Edited by David Braund and John Wilkins. Exeter: University of Exeter Press, 2000.

Breu, Clarissa. *Autorschaft in der Johannesoffenbarung: Eine postmoderne Lektüre*. WUNT 2.541. Tübingen: Mohr Siebeck, 2020.

Brookins, Timothy A. "The Alleged 'Letter Allegedly from Us': The Parallel Function of ὡς δι' ἡμῶν in 2 Thessalonians 2.2." *JSNT* 45.1 (2022): 109–131.

Brookins, Timothy A. "'I Rather Appeal to *Auctoritas*': Roman Conceptualization of Power and Paul's Appeal to Philemon." *CBQ* 77.2 (2015): 302–321.

Bruce, Frederick F. *1 & 2 Thessalonians*. World Books Commentaries 45. Waco, TX: World Books, 1982.

Burini, Clara. *Lettera ai Filippesi; Martirio*. Bologna: EDB, 1998.

Burke, Seán. *The Death and Return of the Author: Criticism and Subjectivity in Barthes, Foucault, and Derrida*. Edinburgh: Edinburgh University Press, 1992.

Burke, Seán. "The Ethics of Signature." Pages 237–244 in *Language and the Subject*. Edited by Karl Simms. Critical Studies 9. Amsterdam: Rodopi, 1997.

Candida R. Moss. "The Secretary: Enslaved Workers, Stenography, and the Production of Early Christian Literature." *JTS* 74.1 (2023): 20–56.

Carriker, Andrew. *The Library of Eusebius of Caesarea*. VCSupp 67. Leiden: Brill, 2003.

Chalmers, Matthew. "Past Paul's Jewishness: The Benjaminite Paul in Epiphanius of Cyprus." *HTR* 115.3 (2022): 309–330.

Clark, Elizabeth A. and Diane F. Hatch. *The Golden Bough, the Oaken Cross: The Virgilian Cento of Faltonia Betitia Proba*. Texts and Translations 5. Chico, CA: Scholars Press, 1981.

Collins, John J. *Between Athens and Jerusalem: Jewish Identity in the Hellenistic Diaspora*. Grand Rapids, MI: Eerdmans, 2000.

Concannon, Cavan. *Assembling Early Christianity: Trade, Networks, and the Letters of Corinth*. Cambridge: Cambridge University Press, 2017.

Concannon, Cavan. *Profaning Paul*. Class 200. Chicago, IL: University of Chicago Press, 2021.

Coogan, Jeremiah. *Eusebius the Evangelist: Rewriting the Fourfold Gospel in Late Antiquity*. Cambridge: Cambridge University Press, 2022.

Coogan, Jeremiah. "Gospel as Recipe Book: Nonlinear Reading and Practical Texts in Late Antiquity." *EC* 12.1 (2021): 40–60.

Coogan, Jeremiah. "Imagining Gospel Authorship: Anonymity, Collaboration, and Monography in a Pluriform Corpus." Pages 203–223 in *Authorial Fictions and Attributions in the Ancient Mediterranean*. Edited by Chance E. Bonar and Julia D. Lindenlaub. WUNT II 609. Tübingen: Mohr Siebeck, 2024.

Coogan, Jeremiah. "Meddling with the Gospel: Celsus, Early Christian Textuality, and the Politics of Reading." *NT* 65.3 (2023): 400–422.

Coogan, Jeremiah. "Reading (in) a Quadriform Cosmos: Gospel Books and the Early Christian Bibliographic Imagination." *JECS* 31 (2023): 85–103.

Coogan, Jeremiah and Jacob A. Rodriguez. "Ordering Gospel Textuality in the Second Century." *JTS* 74.1 (2023): 57–102.

Countryman, Louis William. "Tertullian and the Regula Fidei." *The Second Century* 2.4 (1982): 208–227.

Cranfield, Charles E. B. "Changes of Person and Number in Paul's Epistles." Pages 280–289 in *Paul and Paulinism: Essays in Honour of C. K. Barrett*. Edited by Morna D. Hooker and Stephen G. Wilson. London: SPCK Press, 1982.

Cribiore, Raffaella. *Gymnastics of the Mind: Greek Education in Hellenistic and Roman Egypt*. Princeton, NJ: Princeton University Press, 2005.

Cueva, Edmund P. and Javier Martínez, ed. *Splendide Mendax: Rethinking Fakes and Forgeries in Classical, Late Antique, and Early Christian Literature*. Groningen: Barkhuis, 2016.

Cullhed, Sigrid Schottenius. "In Bed with Virgil: Ausonius' *Wedding Cento* and Its Reception." *Greece & Rome* 63.2 (2016): 237–250.

Daniélou, Jean. *Message évangélique et culture hellénistique aux IIe et IIIe siècles*. Tournai: Desclée & Cie., 1961.

DeVore, David. "Character and Convention in the Letters of Eusebius' *Ecclesiastical History*." *JECS* 7.2 (2014): 233–252.

Dhont, Marieke. "Greek Education and Cultural Identity in Greek-Speaking Judaism: The Jewish-Greek Historiographers." *Journal for the Study of the Pseudepigrapha* 29.4 (2020): 217–228.

Ehrman, Bart D. *Forgery and Counterforgery: The Use of Literary Deceit in Early Christian Polemics*. Oxford: Oxford University Press, 2013.

Ellis, Edward E. *Prophecy and Hermeneutic in Early Christianity: New Testament Essays*. WUNT 18. Tübingen: Mohr Siebeck, 1978.

Elsner, Jaś. "Late Narcissus: Classicism and Culture in a Late Roman Cento." Pages 176–204 in *The Poetics of Late Latin Literature*. Edited by Jaś Elsner and Jesús Hernández Lobato. Oxford: Oxford University Press, 2017.

Favrelle, Geneviève. *Eusèbe de Césarée, La Préparation Évangélique*. SC 292. Paris: Cerf, 1982.

Fee, Gordon D. *The First and Second Letters to the Thessalonians*. NICNT. Grand Rapids, MI: Eerdmans, 2009.

Fee, Gordon D. *The First Epistle to the Corinthians*. Grand Rapids, MI: Eerdmans, 1987.

Fehling, Detlev. *Herodotus and His "Sources": Citation, Invention, and Narrative Art*. Translated by J. G. Howie. ARCA 21. Leeds: Francis Cairns, 1989.

Feldman, Louis H. *Jew and Gentile in the Ancient World*. Princeton, NJ: Princeton University Press, 1992.

Ferguson, Everett. "Irenaeus's *Proof of the Apostolic Preaching* and Early Catechetical Instruction." Pages 1–17 in *The Early Church at Work and Worship*, Vol. 2. Edited by Everett Ferguson. Eugene: Wipf & Stock, 2014.

Fewster, Gregory P. "'Can I Have Your Autograph?': On Thinking about Pauline Authorship and Pseudepigraphy." *Bulletin for the Study of Religion* 43.3 (2014): 30–39.

Foucault, Michel. "What Is an Author?" Pages 205–222 in *Aesthetics, Method, and Epistemology*. Edited by James D. Faubion and Translated by Robert Hurley. New York: New Press, 1998.

Fournet, Jean-Luc. "Une éthopée de Caïn dans le Codex des Visions de la Fondation Bodmer." *ZPE* 92 (1992): 253–266.

Fowler, Kimberley A. "Divine Authorship and Variations of Pseudepigraphy in the Second Discourse of Great Seth and the Wisdom of Jesus Christ." *EC* 14.4 (2023): 446–461.

Frey, Jörg. "Das Corpus Johanneum und die Apokalypse des Johannes: Die Johanneslegende, die Probleme der johanneischen Verfasserschaft und die Frage der Pseudonymität der Apokalypse." Pages 71–133 in *Poetik und Intertextualität der Johannesapokalypse*. Edited by Stefan Alkier, Thomas Hieke, and Tobias Nicklas. WUNT 346. Tübingen: Mohr Siebeck, 2015.

Furnish, Victor P. *II Corinthians*. Anchor Bible 32A. Garden City: Doubleday Press, 1984.

Genette, Gérard. *Narrative Discourse: An Essay in Method*. Translated by Jane E. Lewin. Ithaca, NY: Cornell University Press, 1980.

Genette, Gérard. *Palimpsests: Literature in the Second Degree*, Stages 8. Lincoln: University of Nebraska Press, 1997.

Genette, Gérard. *Paratexts: Thresholds of Interpretation*. Literature, Culture, Theory 20. Cambridge: Cambridge University Press, 2009.

Geue, Tom. *Author Unknown: The Power of Anonymity in Ancient Rome*. Cambridge, MA: Harvard University Press, 2019.

Given, James Gregory. "Utility and Variance in Late Antique Witnesses to the Abgar-Jesus Correspondence." *Archiv für Religionsgeschichte* 17.1 (2016): 187–222.

Goulder, Michael D. "Silas in Thessalonica." *JSNT* 48 (1992): 87–106.

Goulet, Richard. "Les références chez Diogène Laërce: sources ou autorités?" Pages 149–166 in *Titres et Articulations du Text dans les Oeuvres Antiques: Actes du Colloque International de Chantilly 13–15 décembre 1994*. Edited by Jean-Claude Fredouille, Marie-Odile Goulet-Cazé, Philippe Hoffmann, et al. Paris: Institut d'Études Augustiniennes, 1997.

Grant, Robert M. *Irenaeus of Lyons*. London: Routledge, 1997.

Gray, Vivienne. "Interventions and Citations in Xenophon, *Hellenica* and *Anabasis*." *CQ* 53.1 (2003): 111–123.

Gray, Vivienne. "Thucydides' Source Citations: 'It Is Said'." *CQ* 61.1 (2011): 75–90.

Green, Roger P. H. *Decimi Magni Ausonii Opera*. Oxford: Clarendon, 1999.

Green, Roger P. H. "Proba's Cento: Its Date, Purpose, and Reception." *CQ* 45.2 (1995): 551–563.

Gruen, Erich S. *Fragmentary Jewish Historians and Biblical History*. Göttingen: Vandenhoeck & Ruprecht, 2019.

Hanson, Ann E. "Galen: Author and Critic." Pages 22–53 in *Editing Texts*. Edited by Glenn W. Most. Aporemata 2. Göttingen: Vandenhoeck & Ruprecht, 1998.

Hardie, Philip. *Classicism and Christianity in Late Antique Latin Poetry*. Sather Classical Lectures 74. Oakland: University of California Press, 2019.

Harnack, Adolf von. *Die Briefsammlung des Apostels Paulus, und die anderen vorkonstantinischen christlichen Briefsammlungen: Sechs Vorlesungen aus der altkirchlichen Literaturegeschicthe*. Leipzig: J. C. Hinrich's Buchhandlung, 1926.

Harris, Brendan. "Irenaeus's Engagement with Rhetorical Theory in His Exegesis of the Johannine Prologue in *Adversus Haereses* 1.8.5–1.9.3." *VC* 72 (2018): 405–420.

Hartog, Paul. *Polycarp's Epistle to the Philippians and the Martyrdom of Polycarp: Introduction, Text, and Commentary*. Oxford: Oxford University Press, 2013.

Heckel, Theo K. "Die Historisierung der johannischen Theologie im Ersten Johannesbrief." *NTS* 50 (2004): 425–443.

Hengel, Martin. *Die Evangelienüberschriften*. SHWPH 1984.3. Heidelberg: C. Winter, 1984.

Hilberg, Isidorus, ed. *Sancti Eusebii Hieronymi Epistulae, Pars I: Epistulae I–LXX*. CSEL 54. Vienna: Tempsky, 1918.

Holladay, Carl R. *Fragments from the Hellenistic Jewish Authors. Volume I: Historians*. Chico, CA: Scholars, 1983.

Holladay, Carl R. *Fragments from the Hellenistic Jewish Authors. Volume II: Poets*. Chico, CA: Scholars, 1989.

Holladay, Carl R. *Fragments from the Hellenistic Jewish Authors. Volume III: Aristobulus*. Chico, CA: Scholars, 1995.

Holladay, Carl R. *Hellenistic Jewish Literature and the New Testament*. Edited by Jonathan M. Potter and Michael K. W. Suh. WUNT 468. Tübingen: Mohr Siebeck, 2021.

Hopkins, John North and Scott McGill, ed. *Forgery beyond Deceit: Fabrication, Value, and the Desire for Ancient Rome*. Oxford: Oxford University Press, 2023.

Hubbard, Moyer V. "Urban Uprising in the Roman World: The Social Setting of Sosthenes." *NTS* 51 (2005): 416–428.

Inowlocki, Sabrina. *Eusebius and the Jewish Authors: His Citation Technique in an Apologetic Context*. Ancient Judaism and Early Christianity 64. Leiden: Brill, 2006.

Jacob, Christian. "Athenaeus the Librarian." Pages 85–110 in *Athenaeus and His World: Reading Greek Culture in the Roman Empire*. Edited by David Braund and John Wilkins. Exeter: University of Exeter Press, 2000.

Jacobs, Andrew. "A Jew's Jew: Paul and the Early Christian Problem of Jewish Origins." *Journal of Religion* 86.2 (2006): 258–286.

Jacobson, Howard. "Artapanus Judaeus." *Journal of Jewish Studies* 57.2 (2006): 210–221.

Jacobson, Howard. "Eusebius, Polyhistor and Ezekiel." *Journal for the Study of the Pseudepigrapha* 15.1 (2005): 75–77.

Jansari, Sushma. "From Geography to Paradoxography: The Use, Transmission and Survival of Megasthenes' *Indica*." *Journal of Ancient History* 8.1 (2020): 26–49.

Janßen, Martina. *Unter falschem Namen: Eine kritische Forschungsbilanz frühchristlicher Pseudepigraphie*. Arbeiten zur Religion und Geschichte des urchristentumss 14. Frankfurt: Peter Lang, 2003.

Janßen, Martina. "'Was ist ein Autor?' Vorstellungen und (Selbst-) Inszenierungen von Autorschaft in der Antike." Pages 49–109 in *Autorschaft und Autorisierungs strategien in apokalyptischen Texten*. Edited by Jörg Frey, Michael R. Jost, and Franz Tóth. WUNT 426. Tübingen: Mohr Siebeck, 2019.

Johnson, Aaron P. *Ethnicity and Argument in Eusebius's Praeparatio evangelica*. Oxford Early Christian Studies. Oxford: Oxford University Press, 2006.

Johnson, William. *Readers and Reading Culture in the High Roman Empire: A Study of Elite Communities*. Oxford: Oxford University Press, 2010.

Joly, Robert. *Le Pasteur: Introduction, Texte Critique, Traduction et Notes*, 2nd ed. SC 53. Paris: Cerf, 1997.

Joost-Gaugier, Christiane L. "The Early Beginnings of the Notion of 'Uomini Famosi' and the 'De Viris Illustribus' in Greco-Roman Literary Tradition." *Artibus et historiae* 3.6 (1982): 97–115.

Jordan, Mark D. *Convulsing Bodies: Religion and Resistance in Foucault*. Stanford, CA: Stanford University Press, 2015.

Karanika, Andromache. "Female Voice, Authorship, and Authority in Eudocia's Homeric Centos." Pages 95–107 in *Fakes and Forgers in Classical Literature: Ergo decipiatur!* Edited by Javier Martínez. Metaphorms 2. Leiden: Brill, 2014.

King, Karen L. "'What Is an Author?' Ancient Author-Function in the *Apocryphon of John* and the Apocalypse of John." Pages 15–42 in *Scribal Practices and Social Structures among Jesus Adherents: Essays in Honour of John S. Kloppenborg.* Edited by William E. Arnal, Richard S. Ascough, Robert A. Derrenbacker Jr., et al. BETL 285. Leuven: Peeters, 2016.

Klauck, Hans-Josef. *1. Korintherbrief.* Neue Echter Bible 7. Würzburg: Echter, 1987.

Knox, Emily. *Book Banning in 21st-Century America.* Lanham, MD: Rowman & Littlefield, 2015.

Lamacchia, Rosa. *Hosidii Getae: Medea Cento Vergilianus.* Leipzig: B. G. Teubner Verlaggesellschaft, 1981.

Lampland, Martha and Susan Leigh Star, ed. *Standards and Their Stories: How Quantifying, Classifying, and Formalizing Practices Shape Everyday Life.* Ithaca, NY: Cornell University Press, 2009.

Larsen, Matthew D. C. "Accidental Publication, Unfinished Texts and the Traditional Goals of New Testament Textual Criticism." *JSNT* 39.4 (2017): 362–387.

Larsen, Matthew D. C. "Correcting the Gospel: Putting the Titles of the Gospels in Historical Context." Pages 78–103 in *Rethinking "Authority" in Late Antiquity: Authorship, Law, and Transmission in Jewish and Christian Tradition.* Edited by Abraham J. Berkovitz and Mark Letteney. Abingdon: Routledge, 2018.

Larsen, Matthew D. C. *Gospels before the Book.* Oxford: Oxford University Press, 2018.

Lefteratou, Anna. *The Homeric Centos: Homer and the Bible Interwoven.* Oxford: Oxford University Press, 2023.

Levine, Caroline. *Forms: Whole, Rhythm, Hierarchy, Network.* Princeton, NJ: Princeton University Press, 2015.

Lofthouse, William F. "'I' and 'We' in the Pauline Letters." *ExpTim* 64.8 (1953): 241–245.

Lofthouse, William F. "Singular and Plural in St. Paul's Letters." *ExpTim* 58 (1947): 179–182.

Lundhaug, Hugo. "Pseudepigraphy and Coptic Apocrypha." *EC* 14.4 (2023): 515–528.

Maciver, Calum Alasdair. "Truth, Narration, and Interpretation in Lucian's *Verae Historiae.*" *American Journal of Philology* 137.2 (2016): 219–250.

Mack, Burton L. *Wisdom and the Hebrew Epic: Ben Sira's Hymn in Praise of the Fathers*. Chicago, IL: University of Chicago Press, 1985.

Malamud, Martha. "Double, Double: Two African Medeas." *RAMUS* 41.1–2 (2012): 161–189.

Malina, Bruce J. *Timothy: Paul's Closest Associate*. Collegeville, MN: Liturgical Press, 2008.

Maltomini, Franco. "P. Lond. 121 (= *PGM VII*), 1–221: Homeromanteion." *ZPE* 106 (1995): 107–122.

Marchal, Joseph A., ed. *After the Corinthian Women Prophets: Reimagining Rhetoric and Power*. Semeia Studies 97. Atlanta, GA: SBL Press, 2021.

Marchal, Joseph A. *Bodies on the Verge: Queering Pauline Epistles*. Atlanta: SBL Press, 2019.

Martens, Peter. "Classifying Early Christian Writings: Boundaries, Arrangements, and Latent Dynamics." *EC* 12 (2021): 431–446.

McGill, Scott. "Tragic Vergil: Rewriting Vergil as a Tragedy in the Cento 'Medea'." *CW* 95.2 (2002): 143–161.

McGill, Scott. *Vergil Recomposed: The Mythological and Secular Centos in Antiquity*. Oxford: Oxford University Press, 2005.

McGill, Scott. "Virgil, Christianity, and the *Cento Probae*." Pages 173–194 in *Texts and Culture in Late Antiquity: Inheritance, Authority, and Change*. Edited by J. H. David Scourfield. Swansea: Classical Press of Wales, 2007.

Meehan, Kasey and Jonathan Friedman. "Banned in the USA: State Laws Supercharge Book Suppression in Schools." *PEN America*. April 20, 2023. https://pen.org/report/banned-in-the-usa-state-laws-supercharge-book-suppression-in-schools/.

Morris, Leon. *The First and Second Epistles to the Thessalonians*. NICNT. Grand Rapids, MI: Eerdmans, 1959.

Moss, Candida. *God's Ghostwriters: Enslaved Christians and the Making of the Bible*. New York: Little, Brown, 2024.

Moss, Candida. "What Large Letters: Invisible Labor, Invisible Disabilities, and Paul's Use of Scribes." Pages 105–122 in *Divided Worlds?: Challenges in Classics and New Testament Studies*. Edited by Caroline Johnson Hodge, Timothy A. Joseph, and Tat-siong Benny Liew. Atlanta, GA: SBL Press, 2023.

Mroczek, Eva. *The Literary Imagination in Jewish Antiquity*. Oxford: Oxford University Press, 2016.

Muehlberger, Ellen. "On Authors, Fathers, and Holy Men." *Marginalia*. September 20, 2015. https://themarginaliareview.com/on-authors-fathers-and-holy-men-by-ellen-muehlberger/.

Murphy, Trevor. *Pliny the Elder's Natural History: The Empire in the Encyclopedia*. Oxford: Oxford University Press, 2014.

Murphy-O'Connor, Jerome. "Co-authorship in the Corinthian Correspondence." *Revue biblique* 100 (1993): 562–579.

Najman, Hindy. *Seconding Sinai: The Development of Mosaic Discourse in Second Temple Judaism*. Supplements to the Journal for the Study of Judaism 77. Leiden: Brill, 2003.

Najman, Hindy and Irene Peirano Garrison. "Pseudepigraphy as an Interpretative Construct." Pages 331–355 in *The Old Testament Apocrypha: Fifty Years of the Pseudepigraphy Section at the SBL*. Edited by Matthias Henze and Liv Ingeborg Lied. Early Judaism and Its Literature 50. Atlanta, GA: SBL Press, 2019.

Nasrallah, Laura Salah. "'Out of Love for Paul': History and Fiction and the Afterlife of the Apostle Paul." Pages 73–96 in *Early Christian and Jewish Narrative: The Role of Religion in Shaping Narrative Forms*. Edited by Ilaria Ramelli and Judith Perkins. Tübingen: Mohr Siebeck, 2015.

Nelles, William. *Frameworks: Narrative Levels and Embedded Narrative*. American University Studies Series 19, General Literature 33. New York: Peter Lang, 1997.

Ní-Mheallaigh, Karen. "The Game of the Name: Onymity and the Contract of Reading in Lucian." Pages 121–132 in *Lucian of Samosata: Greek Writer and Roman Citizen*. Edited by Francesca Mestra and Pilar Gomez. Barcelona: Universitat de Barcelona, 2010.

Olson, Steven Douglas. "Athenaeus' 'Fragments' of Non-fragmentary Prose Authors and Their Implications." *American Journal of Philology* 139.3 (2018): 423–450.

Pagels, Elaine. "Irenaeus, the 'Canon of Truth', and the Gospel of John: 'Making a Difference' through Hermeneutics and Ritual." *VC* 56.4 (2002): 339–371.

Pagels, Elaine. *The Johannine Gospel in Gnostic Exegesis: Heracleon's Commentary on John*. Society of Biblical Literature Monograph Series 17. Nashville, TN: Abingdon Press, 1973.

Peirano Garrison, Irene. "*Ille ego qui quondam*: On Authorial (An)onymity." Pages 251–285 in *The Author's Voice in Classical and Late Antiquity*. Edited by Anna Marmodoro and Jonathan Hill. Oxford: Oxford University Press, 2013.

Peirano Garrison, Irene. *Persuasion, Rhetoric and Roman Poetry*. Cambridge: Cambridge University Press, 2019.

Peirano Garrison, Irene. *The Rhetoric of the Roman Fake: Latin Pseudepigrapha in Context*. Cambridge: Cambridge University Press, 2012.

Pollmann, Karla. "Sex and Salvation in the Vergilian Cento of the Fourth Century." Pages 79–96 in *Romane Memento: Vergil in the Fourth Century*. Edited by Roger Rees. London: Duckworth, 2004.

Prior, Michael. *Paul the Letter-Writer and the Second Letter to Timothy*. JSNTSup 23. Sheffield: Sheffield Academic Press, 1989.

Reece, Steve. *Paul's Large Letters: Paul's Autographic Subscriptions in the Light of Ancient Epistolary Conventions*. London: Bloomsbury, 2017.

Reed, Annette Yoshiko. "Pseudepigraphy, Authorship, and the Reception of 'the Bible' in Late Antiquity." Pages 467–490 in *The Reception and Interpretation of the Bible in Late Antiquity: Proceedings of the Montreal Colloquium in Honour of Charles Kannengiesser, 11–13 October 2006*. Edited by Lorenzo DiTommaso and Lucian Turcescu. Leiden: Brill, 2008.

Refoulé, François. *Traité de la Prescription Contre les Hérétiques*. SC 46. Paris: Cerf, 1957.

Richards, Ernest Randolph. *Paul and First-Century Letter Writing: Secretaries, Composition and Collection*. Downers Grove, IL: InterVarsity Press, 2004.

Richards, Ernest Randolph. *The Secretary in the Letters of Paul*. WUNT 2.42. Tübingen: Mohr Siebeck, 1991.

Richards, Ernest Randolph. "Silvanus Was Not Peter's Secretary: Theological Bias in Interpreting Σιλουανοῦ … ἔγραψα in 1 Peter 5:12." *JETS* 43.3 (2000): 417–432.

Robertson, Paul. "The Polemic of Individualized Appellation in Late Antiquity: Creating Marcionism, Valentinianism, and Heresy." *SLA* 2.2 (2018): 180–214.

Rodenbiker, Kelsie G. "The Second Peter: Pseudepigraphy as Exemplarity in the Second Canonical Petrine Epistle." *NT* 65 (2023): 109–131.

Rousseau, Adelin and Louis Doutreleau, ed. *Irénée de Lyon, Contre les Hérésies Livre I, Tome 2: Texte et traduction*. Paris: Cerf, 1979.

Rousseau, Adelin and Louis Doutreleau, ed. *Irénée de Lyon, Contre les Hérésies Livre III, Tome 2: Texte et traduction*. Paris: Cerf, 1974.

Sandnes, Karl Olav. *The Gospel "According to Homer and Vergil": Cento and Canon*. NT Supp 138. Leiden: Brill, 2011.

Sandnes, Karl Olav. "The Rule of Faith: Getting the Jigsaw Puzzle Right." *Studia Theologica – Nordic Journal of Theology* 77.1 (2023): 1–18.

Sargent, Benjamin. "Chosen through Sanctification (1 Pet 1,2 and 2 Thess 2,13): The Theology or Diction of Silvanus?" *Biblica* 94.1 (2013): 117–120.

Schreiner, Thomas R. *Interpreting the Pauline Epistles*, 2nd ed. Grand Rapids, MI: Baker Academic Press, 2011.

Schroeder, Guy. *Eusèbe de Césarée: La Préparation Évangélique*. SC 215. Paris: Cerf, 1975.

Schroeder, Guy and Édouard des Places. *Eusèbe de Césarée, La Préparation Évangélique*. SC 369. Paris: Cerf, 1991.

Sedlmeier, Florian. "The Paratext and Literary Narration: Authorship, Institutions, Historiographies." *Narrative* 26.1 (2018): 63–80.

Singer, Peter N. "New Light and Old Texts: Galen on His Own Books." Pages 91–131 in *Galen's Treatise* Περὶ Ἀλυπίας *(De indolentia) in Context: A Tale of Resilience*. Edited by Caroline Petit. Studies in Ancient Medicine 52. Leiden: Brill, 2019.

Singer, Peter N. *Selected Works: Galen*. Oxford: Oxford University Press, 1997.

Sowers, Brian P. *In Her Own Words: The Life and Poetry of Aelia Eudocia*. Hellenic Studies 80. Washington, DC: Center for Hellenic Studies, 2020.

Speyer, Wolfgang. *Die literarische Fälschung im heidnischen und christlichen Altertum*. Munich: Beck, 1971.

Sterling, Gregory E. *Historiography and Self-Definition: Josephus, Luke-Acts, and Apologetic Historiography*. Leiden: Brill, 1992.

Stillinger, Jack. *Multiple Authorship and the Myth of Solitary Genius*. Oxford: Oxford University Press, 1991.

Stuckenbruck, Loren T. "The Epistle of Enoch: Genre and Authorial Presentation." *DSD* 17 (2010): 387–417.

Too, Yun Lee. *The Idea of the Library in the Ancient World*. Oxford: Oxford University Press, 2010.

Too, Yun Lee. "The Walking Library: The Performance of Cultural Memories." Pages 111–123 in *Athenaeus and His World: Reading Greek Culture in the Roman Empire*. Edited by David Braund and John Wilkins. Exeter: University of Exeter Press, 2000.

Tóth, Franz. "Autorschaft und Autorisation." Pages 3–48 in *Autorschaft und Autorisierungsstrategien in apokalyptischen Texten*. Edited by Jörg Frey, Michael R. Jost, and Franz Tóth. WUNT 426. Tübingen: Mohr Siebeck, 2019.

Vaught, Curtis and Thomas Lea. *1, 2 Peter, Jude*. Grand Rapids, MI: Zondervan, 1988.

Vayntrub, Jacqueline. "Before Authorship: Solomon and Prov 1:1." *BI* 26 (2018): 182–206.

Waller, Alexis. "The Erotics of Authenticity in New Testament Historiography." ThD dissertation, Harvard Divinity School, 2021.

Walsh, Robyn Faith. "The *Epistle to the Laodiceans* and the Art of Tradition." Pages 13–39 in *Authorial Fictions and Attributions in the Ancient Mediterranean*. Edited by Chance E. Bonar and Julia D. Lindenlaub. Tübingen: Mohr Siebeck, 2024.

Walsh, Robyn Faith. *The Origins of Early Christian Literature: Contextualizing the New Testament within Greco-Roman Literary Culture.* Cambridge: Cambridge University Press, 2021.

Wannamaker, Charles A. *The Epistles to the Thessalonians: A Commentary on the Greek Text.* NIGTC. Grand Rapids, MI: Eerdmans, 1990.

White, Carolinne. *Early Christian Latin Poets.* London: Routledge, 2000.

Whitmarsh, Tim. "An I for an I: Reading Fictional Autobiography." Pages 233–247 in *The Author's Voice in Classical and Late Antiquity.* Edited by Anna Marmodoro and Jonathan Hill. Oxford: Oxford University Press, 2013.

Wilken, Robert L. "The Homeric Cento in Irenaeus, 'Adversus Haereses' I,9,4." *VC* 21 (1967): 25–33.

Wire, Antoinette Clark. *The Corinthian Women Prophets: A Reconstruction through Paul's Rhetoric.* Minneapolis, MN: Fortress Press, 1990.

Wisniewski, Robert. "Pagans, Jews, Christians, and a Type of Book Divination in Late Antiquity." *JECS* 24.4 (2016): 553–568.

Wright III, Benjamin G. and Eva Mroczek. "Ben Sira's Pseudo-Pseudepigraphy: Idealizations from Antiquity to the Early Middle Ages." Pages 213–239 in *Sirach and Its Contexts: The Pursuit of Wisdom and Human Flourishing.* Edited by Samuel A. Adams, Greg Schmidt Goering, and Matthew Goff. JSJ Supp 196. Leiden: Brill, 2021.

Wyrick, Jed. *The Ascension of Authorship: Attribution and Canon Formation in Jewish, Hellenistic, and Christian Traditions.* Harvard Studies in Comparative Literature 49. Cambridge, MA: Harvard University Press, 2004.

For EU product safety concerns, contact us at Calle de José Abascal, 56–1°,
28003 Madrid, Spain or eugpsr@cambridge.org.

www.ingramcontent.com/pod-product-compliance
Ingram Content Group UK Ltd.
Pitfield, Milton Keynes, MK11 3LW, UK
UKHW020435070226
467784UK00021B/416